# Option Strategy Hedging & Risk Management

An In-Depth Article Introducing an
Interactive Analytical Framework for
Hedging Option Strategy Risk

BRIAN JOHNSON

# DISCLAIMER

Information in this article is provided solely for informational and general educational purposes and should not be construed as an offer to sell or the solicitation of an offer to buy securities or to provide investment advice. Option trading has large potential rewards, but also large potential risk. You must be aware of the risks and be willing to accept them in order to invest in the options markets. Do not trade with money you cannot afford to lose. Historical results are not necessarily indicative of future performance.

# COVER IMAGE

The chaos image on the cover is a graphical metaphor for the seemingly stable patterns of price behavior that can suddenly and unexpectedly devolve into chaos, resulting in discrete price and volatility changes as new equilibrium conditions are negotiated by market participants. The red color scheme represents the resulting financial risk that is always lurking beneath the surface, especially for option traders.

# CONTENTS

# INTRODUCTION

Brian Johnson, an investment professional with over 30 years of experience, is the author of three pioneering books on options: 1) *Option Strategy Risk / Return Ratios*, 2) *Exploiting Earnings Volatility,* and 3) *Option Income Strategy Trade Filters.*

His new in-depth (100+ page) article, *Option Strategy Hedging and Risk Management,* presents a comprehensive analytical framework and accompanying spreadsheet tools for managing and hedging option strategy risk. Drawing on his extensive background in option-pricing and on decades of experience in investment management and trading, Brian Johnson developed these practical techniques to hedge the unique and often overlooked risks associated with trading option strategies.

These revolutionary new tools can be applied to any option strategy, in any market environment. *Option Strategy Hedging and Risk Management* is written in a clear, easy-to-understand fashion and explains how to apply market-specific hedging techniques, using several different hedging vehicles.

Created especially for readers who have some familiarity with options, this practical guide begins with a review of position sizing, including a detailed analysis of the implicit assumptions and embedded risks that could have disastrous consequences, particularly for option traders.

Chapter 2 includes a comprehensive description and analysis of the actual option strategy, position model, and trade rules that are used to create real-world option strategy hedges in the subsequent chapters. This is followed by a thorough explanation and a concrete example of how to use futures to hedge option strategy exit risk. Surprisingly, futures are not well understood in the option community and very few traders employ this simple, effective, and *virtually free* hedging tool.

The next two chapters present a common analytical and hedging framework that is used to identify the most cost-effective hedging solutions for an actual option strategy in a real-world market environment. The process used to identify the lowest-cost hedging solution using actual VIX call options is explained in Chapter 4, followed by the same hedging analysis using put options on the underlying security in Chapter 5. All hedging examples in the article use real-time market prices and actual analytical results.

Proprietary research is included in the article to provide validation for the analytical framework. The article was written to be accessible to a wide audience, so very few mathematical formulas are provided in the text. However, several important formulas are included to facilitate the understanding of important concepts, and to provide further research opportunities for inquisitive traders. The article also includes thirty separate graphs and tables to illustrate how the tools can be used in practice.

Perhaps most important, *Option Strategy Hedging and Risk Management* includes a download link to the accompanying Excel spreadsheet with macros designed to perform *all of the position sizing and hedging calculations in the article.* Chapters 1, 3, 4, and 5 all have their own dedicated tabs in the spreadsheet. The data from the article is included in the spreadsheet, which allows the reader to reproduce all of the examples from the article. All of the spreadsheet functions are automated through the use of push-button macros, making spreadsheet operation as simple as possible.

Finally, Chapter 6 examines practical considerations and prospective applications of these innovative new tools.

# 1 - POSITION SIZING

Selling chronically overvalued options is a proven way to generate excess returns. I refer to these types of positions as option income strategies (OIS), due to their income component. If the price of the underlying security remains relatively constant, option income strategies increase in value as time passes. Option income strategies can be market neutral (e.g. iron condors) or market directional (e.g. bull put credit spreads), but all option income strategies have a positive income component by definition.

In my first book (*Option Strategy Risk Return Ratios*), I provided evidence from several different sources that validated the historical edge of trading option income strategies (OIS). In my most recent article (*Option Income Strategy Trade Filters*), I went much further.

I aggregated the results for 15,434 OIS trades, each managed with the same comprehensive set of objective tradable entry and exit rules. The OIS trades were implemented on three equity indices: the Russell 2000 index (RUT), the S&P 500 index (SPX) and the NASDAQ 100 index (NDX). The evidence of a historical trading advantage in the equity indices was overwhelming. Even for a conventional strategy without the benefits of any entry timing filters, the 15,434 OIS trades earned an average return of 3.22% on required capital (after commissions). Furthermore, the trades generated $2.10 of cumulative gains for every $1 of cumulative losses and the winning percentage of the unfiltered trades exceeded 85 percent.

If option selling strategies have enjoyed such a significant trading edge historically, why have so many option traders blown up their accounts? The answer: inadequate risk management.

## Position Sizing

Knowing in advance when and how to exit every trade are critical components of risk management, but having an exit strategy is only part of the solution. Even with an exit plan in place, most traders still take far too much risk. In many cases, they completely overlook the most important step in risk management: determining the appropriate amount of capital to risk on each trade.

Once you determine the amount of capital to risk on a given

trade, you can then use the predetermined maximum trade loss for the specific strategy to calculate the corresponding position size to buy or sell. In other words, the amount of capital at risk, the maximum trade loss, and the corresponding position size are all directly related through a simple mathematical formula - one that far too few traders use in practice.

## Total Capital at Risk (TCAR)

Before we can calculate the position size, we must first determine the appropriate amount of capital to risk on each trade. While there are a number of complex algorithms you could use, let's keep this as simple as possible. Most professional traders risk no more than 1% - 2% of their total capital on an individual trade.

Note, total capital at risk (TCAR) of 1% - 2% does not necessarily mean that the market value of each position only represents 1% - 2% of our total capital. It means that if the trade incurs the maximum loss (discussed in more detail later), then we would lose no more than 1% - 2% of our total trading capital.

For example, if we allocated 10% of our total capital to a given trade (position size) and we incurred the maximum loss of 20% on that capital position, we would lose 2% of our total capital (10% position size X 20% maximum loss on trade = 2% total capital at risk).

It might be easier to look at this example in dollars. If our total capital equaled one million dollars, and we allocated 10% of our total capital to the trade, the resulting position size would be $100,000 ($1,000,000 X 10%). If we suffered the maximum loss of 20% on our $100,000 position, we would incur a loss of $20,000 ($100,000 X 20%). The resulting $20,000 loss would equal 2% of our total capital ($20,000 / $1,000,000).

Limiting losses to only 1% - 2% of total capital on each trade might seem overly conservative, but every trader eventually experiences a series of consecutive losses and it is very difficult to recover from losing a large percentage of your total capital, both emotionally and mathematically.

As you can see in Figure 1.1, it would require a 25% return on your portfolio to recover from a cumulative 20% loss of total capital, which would be difficult, but still possible.

After losing 50% of your total capital, you would need a 100% return on your portfolio to return to break-even. This could take years, even without the psychological baggage of a recent 50% draw-down. Losses in excess of 50% of total capital would be insurmountable for most traders.

To be a successful trader, we must always maintain sufficient capital to recover from our losses.

| Figure 1.1: Return Required to Break-Even | |
| --- | --- |
| Cumulative Loss on Total Capital | Total Portfolio Return Required to Break-Even |
| -5.00% | 5.26% |
| -10.00% | 11.11% |
| -15.00% | 17.65% |
| -20.00% | 25.00% |
| -25.00% | 33.33% |
| -30.00% | 42.86% |
| -40.00% | 66.67% |
| -50.00% | 100.00% |
| -60.00% | 150.00% |
| -70.00% | 233.33% |
| -80.00% | 400.00% |
| -90.00% | 900.00% |
| -100.00% | IMPOSSIBLE ! |

So far, our discussion has been limited to a single trade, but if you had a number of positions and they are were positively correlated (e.g. several OIS trades on various equity indices), then you should also limit your aggregate risk on the entire group of correlated positions. If you would like a rule of thumb, try to risk no more than 5% of your total capital on the positively correlated positions.

The first and most important step in successful trading is using our research, knowledge, experience, insight, and analytical tools to identify a systematic and repeatable market edge. We can then design specific trading strategies to exploit our proven statistical advantage. The key to exploiting this advantage over time is playing the game repeatedly, because the odds are in our favor on every trade. It is analogous to owning a casino in Las Vegas.

Casinos limit the size of each bet to ensure the probabilities work in their favor over time. They want blackjack players betting $25 on each hand and playing for hours and hours at a time. The casino's odds of winning increase dramatically as they play the game repeatedly. They do not want a player to walk in and place a $500,000 wager on a single hand of blackjack, just as we do not want to risk losing 50% of our total capital on a single transaction.

## Calculating Position Size

After deciding judiciously on the appropriate amount of total capital to risk on a given trade (as a percentage of our total capital), we then use this value in conjunction with the maximum percentage loss on the trade to calculate the corresponding position size for the trade. As I explained earlier, there is a specific formula that quantifies the relationship between the total capital at risk (TCAR), the maximum loss (ML) per trade, and the corresponding position size (PS). Two versions of the formula are presented below, followed by the definitions of each variable:

**TCAR = PS x ML**

**PS = TCAR / ML**

**TCAR** = Total Capital at Risk: the percentage of our total capital that we could lose by exiting at the predetermined maximum loss

**PS** = Position Size expressed as a percentage of total capital: the market or notional value of the position divided by the total market value of our entire portfolio

**ML** = Maximum Loss on the Trade: percentage loss on the trade if we exit the trade for the maximum loss at the predetermined exit level

## Position Size Relationships

Given our formula for position size (PS = TCAR / ML), it is clear that changes in the total capital at risk (TCAR) and the maximum loss (ML) amount both directly affect the maximum position size (PS). As the total capital at risk (numerator) increases, the position size increases accordingly. However, many traders do not realize that their maximum position size must shrink if they accept a larger maximum loss per trade (denominator) - holding total capital at risk constant. This can be seen in the graph in Figure 1.2 below.

The horizontal (independent) or x-axis represents the total capital at risk (TCAR) per trade. The maximum position size (expressed as a percentage of total capital) is shown on the vertical (dependent) or y-axis. This total capital at risk is determined in advance by the trader. In theory, so is the maximum percentage loss per trade. Together these two independent variables determine the maximum position size.

Each upward-sloping line depicts the position size (as a percentage of total capital) for a given maximum loss level: a 5% maximum loss per trade for the top line, increasing to a 100% maximum loss for the bottom line. For a given level of total capital at risk, the maximum position size decreases as the maximum loss per trade increases. This is equivalent to moving vertically down the chart from line to line.

Similarly, for a given level of total capital at risk, the maximum position size increases as the maximum loss per trade decreases. This is equivalent to moving vertically up the chart from line to line.

Finally, for a given maximum loss per trade, increasing the total capital at risk would increase the position size. This is equivalent to moving from left to right on the chart, remaining on the same line. The upward sloping lines illustrate the direct linear relationship between total capital at risk and position size.

The chart in Figure 1.2 makes it easy to see the relationships between total capital at risk, maximum loss per trade, and position size. However, the table in Figure 1.3 makes it easier to identify the specific values for each variable in the position size formula.

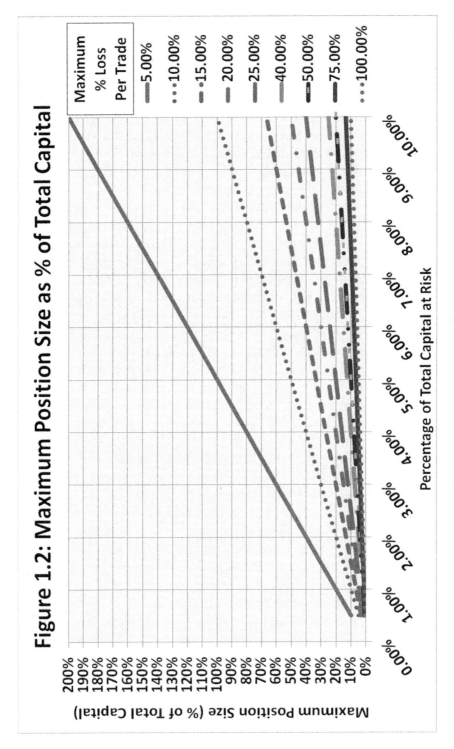

Figure 1.2: Maximum Position Size as % of Total Capital

## Position Size Examples

Let's revisit the numerical example that I used earlier in this chapter. If we were willing to risk losing 2% of our total capital on a given trade and the maximum loss we could incur before exiting that trade was 20%, we could allocate a maximum of 10% of our total capital to the position (2% TCAR/ 20% ML = 10% PS). The resulting 10% position size can be seen at the intersection of the 20% ML column and the 2% TCAR row in Figure 1.3.

If we were willing to risk losing 5% of our total capital on a group of positively correlated trades and the maximum loss on all of those trade was 20%, we could allocate a maximum of 25% of our total capital to the aggregate position (5% TCAR/ 20% ML = 25% PS). The resulting 25% position size can be seen at the intersection of the 20% ML column and the 5% TCAR row in Figure 1.3.

| Figure 1.3: Maximum Position Size as % of Total Capital | | | | | | | | | |
|---|---|---|---|---|---|---|---|---|---|
| | Maximum Percentage Loss Per Trade | | | | | | | | |
| | 5.00% | 10.00% | 15.00% | 20.00% | 25.00% | 40.00% | 50.00% | 75.00% | 100.00% |
| 0.50% | 10.00% | 5.00% | 3.33% | 2.50% | 2.00% | 1.25% | 1.00% | 0.67% | 0.50% |
| 1.00% | 20.00% | 10.00% | 6.67% | 5.00% | 4.00% | 2.50% | 2.00% | 1.33% | 1.00% |
| 1.50% | 30.00% | 15.00% | 10.00% | 7.50% | 6.00% | 3.75% | 3.00% | 2.00% | 1.50% |
| 2.00% | 40.00% | 20.00% | 13.33% | 10.00% | 8.00% | 5.00% | 4.00% | 2.67% | 2.00% |
| 2.50% | 50.00% | 25.00% | 16.67% | 12.50% | 10.00% | 6.25% | 5.00% | 3.33% | 2.50% |
| 3.00% | 60.00% | 30.00% | 20.00% | 15.00% | 12.00% | 7.50% | 6.00% | 4.00% | 3.00% |
| 3.50% | 70.00% | 35.00% | 23.33% | 17.50% | 14.00% | 8.75% | 7.00% | 4.67% | 3.50% |
| 4.00% | 80.00% | 40.00% | 26.67% | 20.00% | 16.00% | 10.00% | 8.00% | 5.33% | 4.00% |
| 4.50% | 90.00% | 45.00% | 30.00% | 22.50% | 18.00% | 11.25% | 9.00% | 6.00% | 4.50% |
| 5.00% | 100.00% | 50.00% | 33.33% | 25.00% | 20.00% | 12.50% | 10.00% | 6.67% | 5.00% |
| 5.50% | 110.00% | 55.00% | 36.67% | 27.50% | 22.00% | 13.75% | 11.00% | 7.33% | 5.50% |
| 6.00% | 120.00% | 60.00% | 40.00% | 30.00% | 24.00% | 15.00% | 12.00% | 8.00% | 6.00% |
| 6.50% | 130.00% | 65.00% | 43.33% | 32.50% | 26.00% | 16.25% | 13.00% | 8.67% | 6.50% |
| 7.00% | 140.00% | 70.00% | 46.67% | 35.00% | 28.00% | 17.50% | 14.00% | 9.33% | 7.00% |
| 7.50% | 150.00% | 75.00% | 50.00% | 37.50% | 30.00% | 18.75% | 15.00% | 10.00% | 7.50% |
| 8.00% | 160.00% | 80.00% | 53.33% | 40.00% | 32.00% | 20.00% | 16.00% | 10.67% | 8.00% |
| 8.50% | 170.00% | 85.00% | 56.67% | 42.50% | 34.00% | 21.25% | 17.00% | 11.33% | 8.50% |
| 9.00% | 180.00% | 90.00% | 60.00% | 45.00% | 36.00% | 22.50% | 18.00% | 12.00% | 9.00% |
| 9.50% | 190.00% | 95.00% | 63.33% | 47.50% | 38.00% | 23.75% | 19.00% | 12.67% | 9.50% |
| 10.00% | 200.00% | 100.00% | 66.67% | 50.00% | 40.00% | 25.00% | 20.00% | 13.33% | 10.00% |

*Percentage of Total Capital at Risk* (row axis label)

## The OSHRM Spreadsheet

I provided the position sizing formulas and examples because it is important for all traders to understand the relationships between total capital at risk (TCAR), maximum loss (ML) per trade, and position size (PS). I also provided an Excel spreadsheet that is included with the purchase of this article that performs all of the position size calculations as well as the hedging analysis explained in subsequent chapters. The single user license for the OSHRM spreadsheet that accompanies this article is not transferable. Instructions for downloading the accompanying spreadsheet are in the Resources section at the end of the article.

Users may only enter or modify values in spreadsheet cells with a solid-blue background and white type. Most of the other cells are protected and may not be changed by the user. In addition, data validation rules apply to many cell values to preserve the integrity and validity of the calculations.

In addition to modifying the values in cells with blue backgrounds, users may also use the macro buttons to execute macro functions. Access to the Excel VBA (Visual Basic for Applications) code and formulas is restricted, but many formulas and relationships are explained in the text of this article.

The OSHRM workbook has six tabs: Terms, Holidays, PositionSize, FuturesHedge, VIXCallHedge, and EQPutHedge. The Terms tab includes a partial disclaimer and a link to the full terms and conditions on the TraderEdge.Net site that govern the use of the spreadsheet. The user must read and agree to all of the terms and conditions before using the workbook. The workbook will not function unless the terms and conditions have been explicitly accepted.

Until those terms are explicitly accepted, many spreadsheet cells will appear to contain errors: "#VALUE!" These are not spreadsheet errors. The macros and spreadsheet calculations will not function correctly until the terms have been explicitly accepted. The "#VALUE!" messages can also occur when first opening the spreadsheet. If these "#VALUE!" messages ever occur (for any reason), accept the terms on the Terms tab *and then enter a new (different) value in one or more of the blue user input cells to force all of the "#VALUE!" cells to recalculate.* If these steps do not resolve the problem, the error is probably data-specific.

The second tab is named *Holidays* and is self-explanatory. The user enters exchange holidays on this tab to ensure accurate trade-day calculations for the futures and options hedging tabs that we will explore in later chapters. Exchange holidays from 2012 to 2019 are included with the original OSHRM spreadsheet, but it is the user's responsibility to verify the accuracy of the dates, as well as the validity of all calculations provided in the spreadsheet. The spreadsheet is only provided for educational purposes.

The *PositionSize* worksheet is the third tab of the workbook. This worksheet automates the position size formulas discussed in this chapter and can be used interactively by the user to experiment with various combinations of total capital at risk (TCAR) and maximum loss (ML) per trade.

It is always challenging to explain how to use a spreadsheet in a written document. To facilitate the explanation, the first spreadsheet example in Figure 1.4 uses the same values from the first position size calculation example that we reviewed earlier in this chapter (2% TCAR/ 20% ML = 10% PS).

Figure 1.4 is a screenshot of the interactive table on the *PositionSize* tab of the workbook. As you will recall, the cells with the solid-blue background are used to enter values into the spreadsheet. The top half of the table is used to calculate position size and the bottom half of the table is used to evaluate the impact of specific combinations of trade performance and position size.

Let's begin with the top half of the table. As I mentioned earlier, Figure 1.4 uses the same values from the first position size calculation example. However, to provide additional insight, the example also includes the user's total dollar amount of trading capital (B4), which allows all percentage values to be reported in dollars as well (column J). In this example, I assume one million dollars in total capital (B4), which makes the resulting dollar values more intuitive.

In our earlier example, we assumed total capital at risk of 2% (B5) and a maximum loss on the trade of 20% (B6). Based on these input values, the resulting position size (10%) is reported in cell B7. Note, this is a calculated value (no blue background), not an input value. The respective *dollar amounts* of total capital at risk (TCAR), maximum loss on trade (ML), and position size (PS) are calculated in cells J5:J7. All of the values in the earlier Figure 1.3 can be replicated using the interactive tools on the position tab of the spreadsheet.

The bottom half of the table can be used as a tool for scenario or "What If Analysis." In other words, the *actual* total percentage of capital lost (B11) can be calculated from the input values: *actual* percentage loss on trade (B9) and *actual* position size (B10). As was the case above, the respective dollar amounts for each of these values is reported in column J (J9:J11). The same total capital amount (B4) was used in these calculations (one million dollars).

In this "What If" example, I assumed the same *actual* loss on trade (B9) that we used in the position size calculation (B6). However, these cells are not linked. You may enter different values in the bottom half of the table. Instead of using the 10% maximum position size calculated in the top half of the table (B7), I wanted to simulate the impact of exceeding the maximum position size. As a result, I increased the *actual* position size from 10% to 20% (B10). As we would expect, the *actual* percentage of total capital lost would double from 2% (B5) to 4% (B11) due to the increase in *actual* position size from 10% (B7) to 20% (B10).

| | A | B | C | D | E | F | G | H | I | J |
|---|---|---|---|---|---|---|---|---|---|---|
| 1 | | Copyright © 2017 Trading Insights, LLC. All Rights Reserved. | | | | | | | | |
| 2 | | Figure 1.4: Position Size Calculation & What If Analysis | | | | | | | | |
| 3 | | Value | Position Size Calculation | | | | | | | Dollar Value |
| 4 | | 1,000,000 | Total Dollar Amount of Trading Capital (Portfolio Value) | | | | | | | 1,000,000 |
| 5 | | 2.00% | Desired Total Capital At Risk (% of Total Capital) | | | | | | | 20,000 |
| 6 | | 20.00% | Maximum Loss on Trade (% of Position Size) | | | | | | | 20,000 |
| 7 | | 10.00% | Position Size (% of Total Trading Capital Allocated to Trade | | | | | | | 100,000 |
| 8 | | Value | What If Analysis | | | | | | | Dollar Value |
| 9 | | 20.00% | Actual Loss on Trade (% of Position Size) | | | | | | | 40,000 |
| 10 | | 20.00% | Actual Position Size (% of Total Trading Capital) | | | | | | | 200,000 |
| 11 | | 4.00% | Actual Total Capital Lost (% of Total Capital) | | | | | | | 40,000 |

## The Maximum Loss Assumption

If you are an experienced trader, the position size formulas and calculations are probably very familiar. However, very few traders effectively manage the potentially catastrophic risk of the maximum loss assumption hidden in these simple formulas. I will use a second *PositionSize* tab example to demonstrate this risk.

Figure 1.5 is a screenshot of the interactive table on the PositionSize tab of the workbook. We will begin with the position size calculation in the top half of the table, again assuming total capital of one million dollars (B4).

In this example, we will assume total capital at risk of 5% (B5), presumably for a group of OIS trades. We will assume a smaller percentage loss on the trades of only 10% (B6). Based on these input values, the resulting position size of 50% (B7) is significantly larger than our first example (10%), but is still consistent with the framework – provided the underlying assumptions are valid.

The total amount of capital at risk increases (from 2% to 5%) and the maximum loss decreases (from 20% to 10%), both of which increase our maximum position size. We will again use the bottom half of the table to perform a "What If Analysis." Let's assume that we establish a position size equal to 50% (B10) of our total capital, as calculated in the top half of the spreadsheet.

However, this time we will evaluate what would happen if the maximum loss assumption was violated. In other words, instead of being able to exit the group of trades with a maximum loss of 10% (B6), we were not able to exit the trades as planned. Due to a large discrete jump in prices, we would actually lose 100% (B9) of the position size (B10), instead of 10% (B6) of the position size as expected. In this scenario, we would lose 50% (B11) or $500,000 (J11) of our total capital in an instant, far more than our 5% (B5) or $50,000 (J5) desired total capital at risk.

| | Value | Position Size Calculation | Dollar Value |
|---|---|---|---|
| 1 | | Copyright © 2017 Trading Insights, LLC. All Rights Reserved. | |
| 2 | | Figure 1.5: Position Size Calculation & What If Analysis | |
| 3 | Value | Position Size Calculation | Dollar Value |
| 4 | 1,000,000 | Total Dollar Amount of Trading Capital (Portfolio Value) | 1,000,000 |
| 5 | 5.00% | Desired Total Capital At Risk (% of Total Capital) | 50,000 |
| 6 | 10.00% | Maximum Loss on Trade (% of Position Size) | 50,000 |
| 7 | 50.00% | Position Size (% of Total Trading Capital Allocated to Trade | 500,000 |
| 8 | Value | What If Analysis | Dollar Value |
| 9 | 100.00% | Actual Loss on Trade (% of Position Size) | 500,000 |
| 10 | 50.00% | Actual Position Size (% of Total Trading Capital) | 500,000 |
| 11 | 50.00% | Actual Total Capital Lost (% of Total Capital) | 500,000 |

Unfortunately, the actual loss could be even worse. Let's look at a catastrophic scenario. I intentionally did not include a dedicated table for this example. Instead, look back at Figure 1.5 and mentally substitute the new values. This will allow you to assess your understanding of the variable relationships in the position size formulas as we proceed through the example.

What would happen if we used the same scenario in Figure 1.5, except we increased the desired total capital at risk (B5) on a group of correlated trades from 5% to 10%? Risking 10% of our total capital on a group of correlated trades would not be ideal, but it would not be entirely unreasonable. If we did lose 10% of our total capital, it would only require a return of 11.1% to return to break-even (see Figure 1.1). That would certainly be recoverable.

If we risked 10% (B5) of our total capital, what would happen to the calculated position size (B7)? If we used the new calculated position size as the *actual* position size (B10) and incurred the same *actual* loss of 100% (B9) on the group of trades, how much of our total capital would we lose (B11)? Try to determine these values without using the spreadsheet and then use the interactive tools on the *PositionSize* tab to confirm your intuition.

∗∗∗

In the revised scenario above, the maximum position size would increase from 50% to 100% (B7). If we allocated 100% of our capital to the group of trades (B10) and we were unable to exit the trades at our designated 10% stop-loss level (B6) and instead incurred a 100% loss (B9), we would lose 100% of our total capital (B11). Even with a risk management plan in place, one catastrophic event could wipe out our entire portfolio.

## Black-Swan Events

This raises two critical questions: 1) how plausible is the above example and 2) how can we mitigate the risks? There is bad news and good news. The bad news is that the catastrophic example is credible and similar scenarios will eventually occur.

Unfortunately, option income (selling) strategies are particularly vulnerable to large discrete market moves. The principal source of income in option selling strategies is positive Theta. A comprehensive discussion of the Greeks is beyond the scope of this article, but I will briefly define such terms when they are used. For those interested, I provided a very detailed explanation of the Greeks in my first two option books: *Option Strategy Risk Return Ratios* and *Exploiting Earnings Volatility*.

Theta represents the change in the value of an option or option strategy due to the passage of time. Positive Theta means that the value of the option or option strategy will increase over time, holding all of the other variables constant. That certainly does not seem like a problem, but the cost of positive Theta is negative Gamma. In other words, every option strategy that enjoys positive Theta also incurs the risk of negative Gamma.

Rather than focus on an academic definition of Gamma, let's focus on a more intuitive explanation. Negative Gamma means that the decline in the value of the option position is an accelerating function of the change in price. In other words, as the price of the underlying security changes, the value of the option income position will not fall at a constant rate. Instead, it will fall faster and faster. The rate of decline will actually accelerate, as will the resulting losses. Gamma acts on the square of the price change. As a result, if a black swan type event occurred while holding negative Gamma positions, severe (even 100%) losses could result.

How likely are these events? Not very, but they do occur. And we will continue to see them in the future. There are many types of events that could generate catastrophic discrete price changes, such as invasive software viruses that shut down major utilities, market exchanges, communication infrastructure, defense capabilities, or other essential services.

There are also many types of terrorist activities that would have long-term, catastrophic impact on financial markets: disbursement of highly contagious biological agents, use of chemical weapons in population centers, dirty bombs in cities, successful attacks on critical infrastructure, etc.

Geopolitical risks are also ever-present and are becoming increasingly likely with the recent shift toward isolationist and nationalistic values. This increases the risk of unexpected and even unplanned conflicts between nuclear states, which could have long-lasting and catastrophic economic consequences, even without further escalation.

In short, there are an infinite number of different scenarios that could generate black-swan events, most of which we could never even imagine until they actually occur. As I mentioned earlier, black-swan events are extremely unlikely to occur on any given day. However, the cumulative probabilities increase exponentially over time.

A concrete example will allow us to calculate some hypothetical probabilities. Let's assume that the probability of a black-swan event occurring on any given day is only one in one thousand (1/1000). If we assume such events are independent, the probability of one or more black-swan events occurring in the next year would be 30.6%. The probability would jump to 83.9% in five years, 97.4% in 10 years, and 99.9% in twenty years.

Many option income traders deploy new strategies every month. If a catastrophic event occurs anytime in the next one, five, or ten years, they would certainly be exposed. Option income strategies are highly profitable. If we are going to continue to trade these types of strategies and black-swan events will eventually occur, we must develop a plan for mitigating the resulting risks.

The good news is that there are steps we can take to protect our option strategies. In fact, the two principal objectives of this article are to: 1) introduce an analytical framework to manage and control these risks and 2) provide interactive spreadsheet tools to help implement that framework in practice. Chapters Three, Four, and Five of this article are dedicated to these risk management solutions.

To examine these risks and hedging solutions, we will need an actual option income strategy to demonstrate how the spreadsheet tools can be applied in practice. The next chapter will introduce the simple iron condor strategy that will be used in subsequent hedging examples.

# 2 - OPTION STRATEGY EXAMPLE

I selected the iron condor for the upcoming hedging examples because it is arguably one of the purest, simplest, and most representative option income strategies, and one that explicitly exploits the chronic overvaluation of equity index options. In addition, I used the same iron condor strategy in my recent article, *Option Income Strategy Trade Filters*, which provides an in-depth analysis of the iron condor's historical performance metrics. Some of the descriptions and images in this chapter were also used in *Option Income Strategy Trade Filters*. I want to thank Larry Richards and Iota Technologies again for their permission to include screen shots from their software. Figures 2.1 through 2.3 are partial screen capture images from the QuantyCarlo software.

Before describing the iron condor strategy that was used in the hedging examples, I want to emphasize that the analytical framework and hedging tools introduced in this article can be applied to *any option strategy*, not just iron condors. The analytical process and spreadsheet tools are independent of the specific option strategy. However, using a specific strategy in the hedging examples will allow us to use *actual market prices* and realistic market scenarios in all hedging calculations.

## Strategy Construction

Let's start with the basics. What is an iron condor and how is it constructed? It is the combination of two out-of-the-money (OTM) credit spreads: a bear call credit spread and a bull put credit spread.

We will review the out-of-the-money (OTM) bear call credit spread first. "Bear" means bearish, which indicates a strategy that performs well when the price of the underlying security declines. "Call" indicates the strategy is constructed using call options.

17

"Spread" signifies that the strategy requires both the sale and purchase of a call option.

Spreads are covered strategies that explicitly limit the maximum loss of the strategy to a fixed dollar amount that is known at the time the trade is entered. "Credit" spread indicates that the spread results in a cash inflow at the inception of the trade. This also means that we would be entitled to keep this cash inflow if the options we sold expired worthless (this explains the "income" in option income strategies). When originating a credit spread, we sell the option with the higher value and purchase the option of the same type (call or put) with the lower value. This is the source of the credit or inflow. For a call credit spread, we sell the option with the lower strike price and buy the option with the higher strike price.

Finally, the term "out-of-the-money" (OTM) tells us that the strike prices of the options used to construct the credit spread initially have no intrinsic value. In the case of OTM bear call credit spreads, OTM means that the strike prices of the call options are *above* the price of the underlying security when the trade is originated. We sell an OTM call option and buy a call option that is even farther out of the money to limit our losses.

Figure 2.1 is a graphical representation of the payoff diagram for a generic OTM bear call credit spread. You will recall that the "payoff" to the option buyer is also called the intrinsic value and represents the value of exercising in-the-money (ITM) options at expiration. For every positive payoff received by an option buyer, there is a corresponding negative payoff incurred by an option seller.

Remember that the bear call credit spread requires the (short) sale and (long) purchase of an OTM call option. As explained above, the strike price of the long call option purchased will always be above (farther out-of-the-money than) the strike price of the short call option sold.

The payoff function of the OTM bear call credit spread in Figure 2.1 is depicted by three line segments. The first line segment is horizontal and begins at the left-side of the diagram and terminates at the strike price of the short call option. If the price of the underlying security was less than or equal to the strike price of the short call option at expiration, both call options would expire worthless. As a result, the value of the payoff function for the bull call credit spread equals zero for this entire region of the payoff function.

The next linear segment of the payoff function begins at the strike price of the short call option and ends at the strike price of the long call option (moving from left to right). In this region, the slope of the payoff function is negative 1.0 (per share). In other words, for every dollar the price of the underlying security increases in this region (at expiration), the payoff of the bear call credit spread strategy would *decrease* by one dollar (per share).

The third and final horizontal line segment at the right-side of the diagram depicts the payoff function for underlying security prices greater than the strike price of the long call option at expiration. Above this strike price of the *long* call option, the slope of the payoff function is zero. In this region of the payoff function, the short and long call option positions would both be in-the-money at expiration, so any *additional* increase in the price of the underlying security above the strike price of the long call option would not reduce our payoff any further.

When we execute an OTM bear call credit spread, we are a net seller of options. As you can see from the OTM bear call spread payoff diagram in Figure 2.1, the payoff value is always less than or equal to zero. In exchange for accepting the risk of a negative future payoff, we demand a premium when we originate a credit spread trade. In equity index options, the magnitude of the average option premium has historically exceeded the average future payoff, which has generated excess returns for traders of option income strategies.

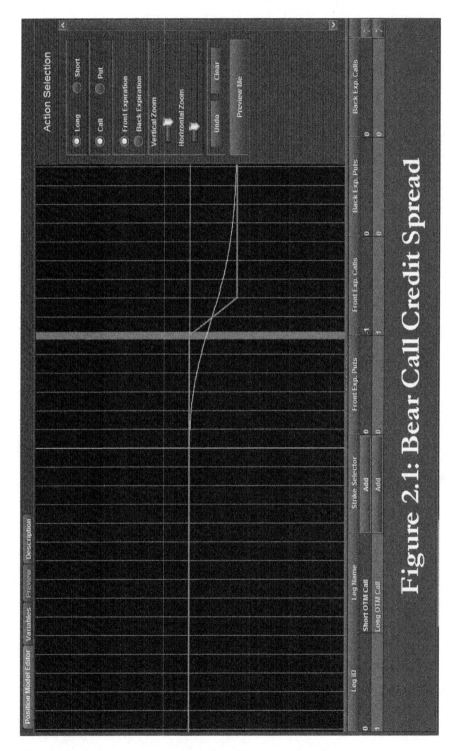

Figure 2.1: Bear Call Credit Spread

## OTM Bull Put Credit Spread

Figure 2.2 is a graphical representation of the payoff diagram of a generic OTM bull put credit spread. "Bull" means bullish, which indicates a strategy that performs well when the price of the underlying security increases. "Put" indicates the strategy is constructed using put options, rather than call options.

However, in the case of OTM bull put credit spreads, OTM means that the strike prices of the put options are *below* the price of the underlying security when the trade is originated. The bull put credit spread requires the (short) sale and (long) purchase of an OTM put option. As explained above, when originating a credit spread, we sell the option with the higher value and purchase the option of the same type with the lower value. We sell an OTM put option and buy a put option that is even farther out of the money to limit our losses. As a result, the strike price of the long put option purchased will be below (farther out-of-the-money than) the strike price of the short put option sold.

The interpretation of the payoff diagram in Figure 2.2 is similar to the interpretation of Figure 2.1, with the same three corresponding payoff line segments. However, put payoff diagrams are intuitively easier to understand when evaluated from right-to-left (OTM to ITM). As was the case in the bear call credit spread example, the payoff (at expiration) for the bull put credit spread is always less than or equal to zero. We must receive compensation for this risk as well, which generates a second source of premium or income for the iron condor strategy.

Figure 2.2: Bull Put Credit Spread

# Iron Condor Strategy

The resulting iron condor strategy is the combination of an OTM bear call credit spread and an OTM bull put credit spread. Option income strategies are designed to be market neutral whenever possible and the iron condor is no exception. The "bear" and "bull" components cancel each other out, resulting in a strategy that experiences very little change in value in response to changes in the price of the underlying security – at least initially.

Directional option strategies with an income component (positive Theta) can also be employed, but the accuracy of the directional entry signal is critical to their success. The hedging tools introduced in the next few chapters can be applied to both directional and non-directional option strategies.

Figure 2.3 shows the payoff diagram for the iron condor strategy, which combines the payoff functions of the OTM bear call credit spread and OTM bull put credit spread into a single payoff function.

For underlying security prices below the strike price of the short put option at expiration (left side of the diagram), the payoff is negative because the short put option expires in the money. Similarly, for underlying security prices above the strike price of the short call option at expiration (right side of diagram), the payoff is also negative because the short call option expires in the money. In the central region of the payoff function (between the strike prices of the short put and call options), the value of the payoff function equals zero because all options expire worthless.

This is the ideal scenario when implementing an iron condor strategy. We want all options to expire worthless. In general, if the realized price change of the underlying security is consistently less than the expected price change of the underlying security, the iron condor strategy will be profitable.

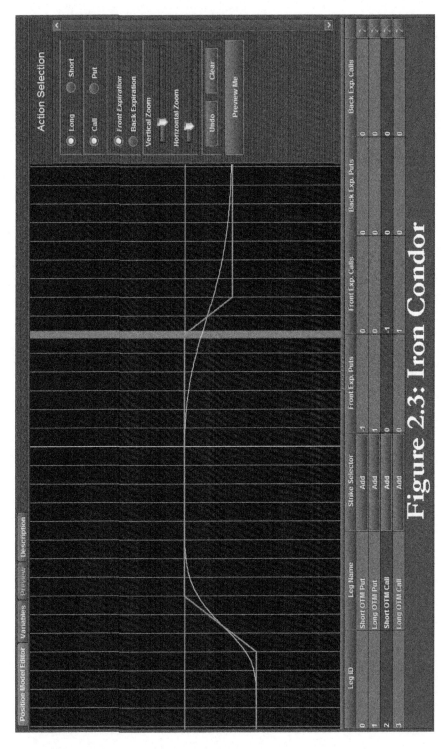

Figure 2.3: Iron Condor

## Asymmetry

You are probably asking yourself a few questions about Figure 2.3. Why does it appear to be asymmetric? Specifically, why is the OTM short put strike price located farther OTM (left) than the short call strike price (right)? And, why is the spread between the put strike prices wider than the spread between the call strike prices? The answer is the vertical volatility skew.

Unfortunately, implied volatility is not constant across strike prices or expiration dates. Volatility modeling is beyond the scope of this article, but volatility skews are very important when selecting the appropriate strike prices and expiration dates for option income strategies. As a result, a brief introduction is required.

The Black-Scholes Option Pricing Model (BSOPM) assumes that volatility is constant and uniform, which is obviously not correct. Historically, equity prices have fallen much more rapidly than they have risen. As a result, equity options with lower strike prices have higher implied volatilities and equity options with higher strike prices have lower implied volatilities.

As a result, when attempting to determine the strike price of an OTM call option one standard deviation (SD) above the current market price, we would need to use a lower implied volatility than when calculating the strike price of an OTM put option one SD below the current market price. The resulting *plus one SD* strike price for the OTM call is closer to the current price of the underlying security than the *minus one SD* strike price for the OTM put. This is called the vertical skew and it answers all of the questions above.

It explains why the strike price of the short put option is farther OTM than the strike price of the short call option, and why the spread between the strike prices of the two put options is wider than the spread between the strike prices of the two call options. In equity index options, the implied volatility of OTM put options is higher than the implied volatility of OTM call options.

If you do not regularly work with the vertical skew and are more familiar with basic option models that ignore volatility skews, the asymmetric shape of the iron condor payoff diagram may seem strange. However, volatility skews are present in the actual market data and should always be integrated into your risk and return assumptions. Failure to incorporate volatility skews when constructing option strategies is one of the most common mistakes made by option traders.

## Iron Condor Position Model

An example of the iron condor position model can be seen at the bottom of Figure 2.3. The first row specifies a short position of one put contract (-1). The second row specifies a long position of one put contract (1) with the same expiration. Together, these two positions make up the OTM bull put credit spread.

Similarly, the third row designates a short position of one call contract (-1). The fourth row designates a long position of one call contract (1), also with the same expiration. Together, these two positions make up the OTM bear call credit spread. The entire four-leg position represents the iron condor position model.

However, you will note that we have not yet explicitly defined which strike price to use for each leg of the iron condor, which is why the "Add" button is shown in the strike selector column for each leg of the position model.

The next section of this chapter will provide a strike selection process used to construct the iron condor hedging examples.

## Position Model – Strike Selection

Figure 2.3 illustrates all aspects of the iron condor position model, except for the strike selectors. There are many different ways to describe which strike price to select for each leg of a position model. One of the most intuitive and most useful strike selectors is Delta targets, which is what I used to create the iron condor position model we will use in the hedging examples.

Delta is the best known and most widely used "Greek" value. A comprehensive discussion of the Greeks is beyond the scope of this article. For a more comprehensive discussion, please refer to dedicated chapters on the Greeks in both of my earlier books (*Option Strategy Risk / Return Ratios* and *Exploiting Earnings Volatility*).

Briefly, Delta represents the change in the value of an option or option strategy for a small change in the price of the underlying security, holding all other variables constant. In other words, it is an instantaneous measure of price sensitivity, but it can also be used as an approximation or proxy for the probability of an option expiring in the money, which is very useful for strategy construction purposes.

This article contains very few formulas, but it is important to understand how and why Delta can be used as a proxy for the probability of an option expiring in the money. Please invest a few extra minutes to study the relationship I describe below. It will pay dividends when constructing your own option strategies.

Delta is actually a term in the Black-Scholes Option Pricing Model (BSOPM). The Delta of a call option (per share) equals N(d1) or the cumulative normal density function of the value d1, which is another term in the BSOPM that quantifies and normalizes the relationship between the strike price and the current price of the underlying security. As mentioned earlier, Delta (or N(d1)) is widely used and reported.

The terms d2 and N(d2) are also used in the BSOPM. N(d2) is *exactly* equal to the probability of an option expiring in the money. Unfortunately, N(d2) is not widely reported, which is why many traders use Delta (N(d1)) as a proxy for the probability of expiring in the money (N(d2)).

This is understandable because d2 equals d1, minus the quantity, sigma times the square root of the time remaining until expiration (in years). In this formula, sigma represents the annualized implied volatility, which is unique to each option. For short-term options in normal volatility environments, Delta is a reasonable proxy for the probability of expiring in the money. To gain some intuition on strategy construction, let's ignore the difference between Delta (N(d1)) and the probability of expiring in the money (N(d2)) and focus on the practical use of Delta as a strike selector. So why is it useful to approximate the probability that each option will expire in the money (ITM)?

Estimating the ITM expiration probabilities allows us to accurately select individual strike prices among options with different implied volatilities. For example, if we wanted to position the short strikes of an iron condor exactly one standard deviation above (short call) and one standard deviation below (short put) the current price of an underlying security, we could use a normal probability table (or Excel NORMDIST function) to find the target Delta. From the NORMDIST function or probability table, we find that 0.16 represents the one-tail probability of an observation falling outside of one-standard deviation.

If we assume Delta is a reasonable proxy for the probability of an option expiring in the money, we would sell the call option with a per-share Delta of 0.16 and sell the put option with a per-share Delta of -0.16. While the Deltas are symmetric, the resulting strike prices of the OTM call and put options would not be symmetric. Why? Because of the asymmetric implied volatilities or vertical skew. This is the beauty of using Deltas to select strikes. Properly calculated, Delta automatically accounts for the differences in implied volatilities for every option in the matrix.

We are finally ready to review the actual Delta targets used to generate the iron condor hedging examples. Unfortunately, one-standard-deviation Delta targets are intuitive, but are suboptimal in practice. Based on my research into theoretical touch-probability advantages (*see Option Strategy Risk Return Ratios* and *Option Income Strategy Trade Filters*), I selected a more appropriate Delta target of plus and minus 0.11 for the short OTM call and put strikes of the iron condor strategy, which corresponds to 1.23 standard deviations above and below the current price of the underlying security.

For the long OTM calls and puts, I used a Delta target of plus and minus 0.08 respectively. I chose the Delta target of plus and minus 0.08 to ensure the resulting long and short strike prices would be different in all price and volatility environments.

To implement the iron condor, we would sell (short) the OTM call and put options with per-share Deltas as close as possible to plus and minus 0.11 respectively. Similarly, we would purchase (establish long positions in) the OTM call and put options with per-share Deltas as close as possible to plus and minus 0.08.

The target Deltas of the long calls and puts were designed to offset, as were the target Deltas of the short calls and puts, resulting in approximately Delta-neutral iron condor trades. In practice, the resulting iron condor is often entered and exited as a single 4-leg spread, although some traders prefer to trade the bull put and bear call spreads individually.

## Specific Iron Condor Position

Now that we have an objective set of rules for constructing an iron condor, we can apply those rules to create a specific iron condor position for use in the upcoming hedging examples. However, to apply our rules in practice, we need an options analytical platform to provide accurate prices and Greek values. I have used OptionVue's software for many years and I will use OptionVue screenshots in each of the remaining chapters. I want to thank Jim Graham and Len Yates at OptionVue again for their permission to include screen shots from their software. Figures 2.4 and 2.5 are partial screen capture images from the OptionVue software

Trading options without a comprehensive option analytical platform is not advisable and the OptionVue software is one of the most powerful tools available. Unlike most broker platforms, OptionVue evaluates both the horizontal and vertical volatility skews and the constant elasticity of volatility (CEV).

The horizontal skew captures the variation in implied volatility as a function of time-to-expiration. The vertical skew measures the variation in implied volatility as a function of strike price. OptionVue's CEV quantifies the change in implied volatility as a function of the change in the price of the underlying security. OptionVue's software incorporates all of these elements into the risk and valuation models, which results in much more realistic risk metrics and valuation forecasts. Please see the resources section at the end of this article for more information about ordering OptionVue's products and services with the Trader Edge discount.

I used OptionVue's matrix *intra-day* on February 27, 2017 to identify the strike prices of the call and put options that were as close as possible to the 0.11 and 0.08 Delta targets discussed earlier in this chapter. I used options on the S&P 500 Index (SPX) to create the iron condor.

The SPX iron condor strategy was constructed with the following four positions:

+40 SPX 2470 APR 17 Calls
- 40 SPX 2460 APR 17 Calls
- 40 SPX 2240 APR 17 Puts
+40 SPX 2210 APR 17 Puts

Figure 2.4 is a partial screen capture of OptionVue's SPX matrix on February 27, 2017. Call options are listed at the top of the image and put options are at the bottom. The strike prices are noted in the far left column. March and April 2017 expirations are shown in the image. The April options on the right side of the Figure 2.4 were used to construct the strategy.

The market price of each option is provided in the first column (MktPr) of each expiration group. The second column (MIV) represents the implied volatility of each option. The iron condor positions are shown in the next column (Ex.Pos). In this case, the values of plus 40 and minus 40 indicate long or short three option contracts, each with a multiplier of 100. The Delta values reported in the next column are expressed per one option contract, which include the 100 multiplier. This is why the option Deltas were almost exactly equal to 100 times the per-share Delta targets presented earlier (0.08 and 0.11). Finally, the time premium or time value of each option is reported in the last column (T.Prem).

According to OptionVue's interpretation of the FINRA Reg-T margin requirements, the capital required to implement this iron condor strategy was $106,712. The iron condor generated a cash *inflow* of $13,228. If the iron condor was held to expiration and all options had expired worthless, the iron condor would have earned $13,228, which would have generated a total return on required capital of 12.40% ($13,228/$106,712 = 12.40%). The trade was originated with 53 calendar days and 38 trade days (not shown) remaining until expiration.

Notice that the per-contract Delta of the long 2,470 calls (8.12) almost exactly offset the Delta of the long 2,210 puts (-8.14) and the Delta of the short 2,460 calls (10.70) nearly offset the Delta of the short 2,240 puts (-11.00). This explains why the iron condor was approximately Delta-neutral at inception.

OptionVue reports the resulting position Greeks at the bottom of their matrix (Figure 2.4). The position Delta was 11.53, which was very small for an iron condor position that required $106,712 dollars in capital. Theta was positive (+194.6) as we would expect at the inception of any option income strategy.

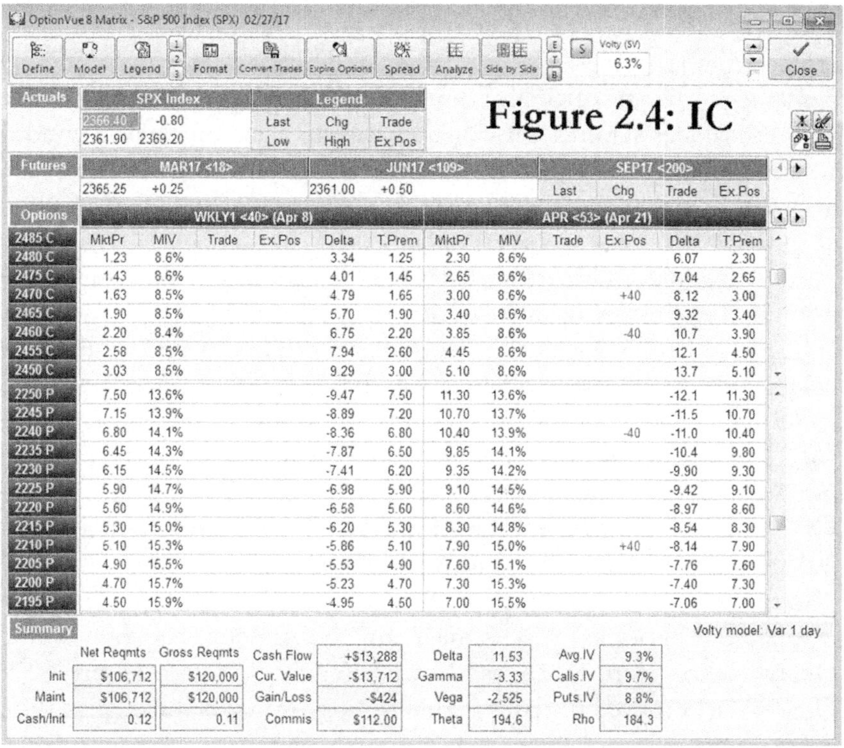

OptionVue 8 Matrix - S&P 500 Index (SPX) 02/27/17

Define | Model | Legend | Format | Convert Trades | Expire Options | Spread | Analyze | Side by Side | Volty (SV) 6.3% | Close

**Figure 2.4: IC**

| Actuals | SPX Index | | Legend | | |
|---|---|---|---|---|---|
| | 2366.40 | -0.80 | Last | Chg | Trade |
| | 2361.90 | 2369.20 | Low | High | Ex.Pos |

| Futures | MAR17 <18> | | JUN17 <109> | | SEP17 <200> | | | |
|---|---|---|---|---|---|---|---|---|
| | 2365.25 | +0.25 | 2361.00 | +0.50 | Last | Chg | Trade | Ex.Pos |

| Options | WKLY1 <40> (Apr 8) | | | | | | APR <53> (Apr 21) | | | | | |
|---|---|---|---|---|---|---|---|---|---|---|---|---|
| 2485 C | MktPr | MIV | Trade | Ex.Pos | Delta | T.Prem | MktPr | MIV | Trade | Ex.Pos | Delta | T.Prem |
| 2480 C | 1.23 | 8.6% | | | 3.34 | 1.25 | 2.30 | 8.6% | | | 6.07 | 2.30 |
| 2475 C | 1.43 | 8.6% | | | 4.01 | 1.45 | 2.65 | 8.6% | | | 7.04 | 2.65 |
| 2470 C | 1.63 | 8.5% | | | 4.79 | 1.65 | 3.00 | 8.6% | | +40 | 8.12 | 3.00 |
| 2465 C | 1.90 | 8.5% | | | 5.70 | 1.90 | 3.40 | 8.6% | | | 9.32 | 3.40 |
| 2460 C | 2.20 | 8.4% | | | 6.75 | 2.20 | 3.85 | 8.6% | | -40 | 10.7 | 3.90 |
| 2455 C | 2.58 | 8.5% | | | 7.94 | 2.60 | 4.45 | 8.6% | | | 12.1 | 4.50 |
| 2450 C | 3.03 | 8.5% | | | 9.29 | 3.00 | 5.10 | 8.6% | | | 13.7 | 5.10 |
| 2250 P | 7.50 | 13.6% | | | -9.47 | 7.50 | 11.30 | 13.6% | | | -12.1 | 11.30 |
| 2245 P | 7.15 | 13.9% | | | -8.89 | 7.20 | 10.70 | 13.7% | | | -11.5 | 10.70 |
| 2240 P | 6.80 | 14.1% | | | -8.36 | 6.80 | 10.40 | 13.9% | | -40 | -11.0 | 10.40 |
| 2235 P | 6.45 | 14.3% | | | -7.87 | 6.50 | 9.85 | 14.1% | | | -10.4 | 9.80 |
| 2230 P | 6.15 | 14.5% | | | -7.41 | 6.20 | 9.35 | 14.2% | | | -9.90 | 9.30 |
| 2225 P | 5.90 | 14.7% | | | -6.98 | 5.90 | 9.10 | 14.5% | | | -9.42 | 9.10 |
| 2220 P | 5.60 | 14.9% | | | -6.58 | 5.60 | 8.60 | 14.6% | | | -8.97 | 8.60 |
| 2215 P | 5.30 | 15.0% | | | -6.20 | 5.30 | 8.30 | 14.8% | | | -8.54 | 8.30 |
| 2210 P | 5.10 | 15.3% | | | -5.86 | 5.10 | 7.90 | 15.0% | | +40 | -8.14 | 7.90 |
| 2205 P | 4.90 | 15.5% | | | -5.53 | 4.90 | 7.60 | 15.1% | | | -7.76 | 7.60 |
| 2200 P | 4.70 | 15.7% | | | -5.23 | 4.70 | 7.30 | 15.3% | | | -7.40 | 7.30 |
| 2195 P | 4.50 | 15.9% | | | -4.95 | 4.50 | 7.00 | 15.5% | | | -7.06 | 7.00 |

Summary — Volty model: Var 1 day

| | Net Reqmts | Gross Reqmts | | | | | | |
|---|---|---|---|---|---|---|---|---|
| | | | Cash Flow | +$13,288 | Delta | 11.53 | Avg.IV | 9.3% |
| Init | $106,712 | $120,000 | Cur. Value | -$13,712 | Gamma | -3.33 | Calls.IV | 9.7% |
| Maint | $106,712 | $120,000 | Gain/Loss | -$424 | Vega | -2,525 | Puts.IV | 8.8% |
| Cash/Init | 0.12 | 0.11 | Commis | $112.00 | Theta | 194.6 | Rho | 184.3 |

Based on the reported position Theta, the value of the iron condor would have initially increased in value by $194.60 per day, holding all of the other variables constant. As explained earlier, there is no free lunch for positive Theta positions. Every positive Theta position has negative Gamma (using conventional Greek calculations) and this iron condor is no exception. The initial Gamma was -3.33. I explained Delta, Theta, and Gamma earlier in this article, but I did not review Vega.

Vega represents the change in the value of an option or option strategy for a one percent increase in implied volatility. Many option income strategies have negative Vega, but calendar spreads are one notable exception. Our example iron condor had an initial position Vega of negative 2,525, indicating that the value of the iron condor would have declined by $2,525 in response to a one percent instantaneous increase in implied volatility, holding all other variables constant.

Figure 2.5 is a screen capture image of OptionVue's graphical analysis screen at the inception of our example iron condor trade on

February 27, 2017. The paired values on the x-axis of the chart represent the price of SPX (the underlying security) and the percentage change of SPX from the initial value of $2,366.40. The left vertical axis signifies the dollar change in value of the iron condor strategy. The right vertical axis denotes the change in the value of the iron condor strategy, expressed as a percentage of the required capital.

The five lines on the chart illustrate the changes in the value of the iron condor strategy on five specific dates: T+0, T+13, T+27, T+40, and T+53. In this case, "T" stands for the trade or entry date. The values of 0, 13, 27, 40, and 53 indicate the number of calendar days in the future. The T+0 line always represents the entry date and the solid line always denotes the expiration date of the shortest-dated option used to construct the strategy. In this case, the T+53 line represents the expiration date of the April 2017 options (April 21, 2017) used to implement the iron condor strategy.

You will notice that the shape of the actual iron condor example in Figure 2.5 looks very similar to the generic version of the QuantyCarlo iron condor shown in the earlier Figure 2.3. QuantyCarlo is used for backtesting option strategies, but OptionVue is an interactive tool to manage option positions in real time. As a result, there is a lot more detail on OptionVue's graphical analysis screen.

As explained earlier, the condor strategy diagram looks unbalanced or asymmetric, especially if you focus on the wings of the diagram. However, instead of concentrating on the wings, look at the center section of the diagram in the immediate vicinity of the initial SPX price of $2,366.40. Notice how flat and uniform the T+0 line is around the $2,366.40 SPX price level. That is what a Delta-neutral strategy looks like and this should be your goal when you implement market-neutral option income strategies.

OptionVue continuously re-estimates the volatility skews and CEV values and uses the latest volatility model parameters to forecast the current and future position values as a function of changes in the price of the underlying security, SPX in this case. The same risk and valuation models are used to estimate the position Greek values as a function of the price of the underlying security.

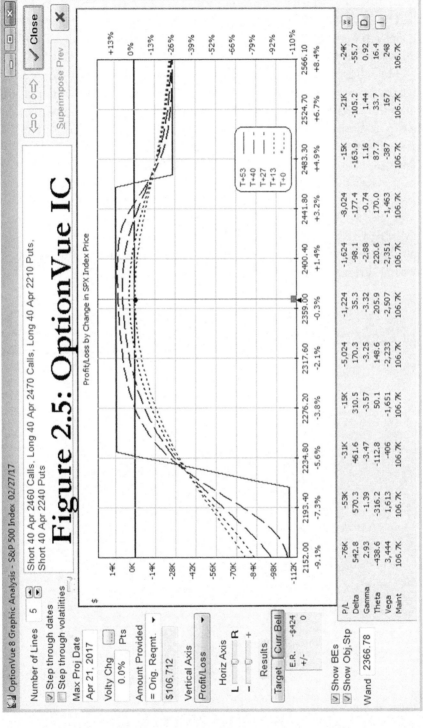

Figure 2.5: OptionVue IC

In practice, the user can click on the desired time period (T+0, T+13, T+27, T+40, and T+53), to control which values are reported in the table at the bottom of the matrix. The values for the T+0 line are shown in Figure 2.5.

This illustrates a critical point: option positions are inherently dynamic, not static. Option prices, profits, implied volatilities, volatility skews, and the Greeks are all changing continuously, often in a non-linear fashion. In order to quantify, manage, and hedge the risk of our option strategies, we need to use a real-time analytical platform that is able to encapsulate realistic option behavior.

We will use OptionVue's graphical analysis tool repeatedly in the next few chapters to provide the required input values for the interactive hedging tools in the accompanying spreadsheet (OSHRM.xlsm). These examples will demonstrate practical risk-management hedging techniques in actual market conditions using several different types of hedging instruments.

# 3 - HEDGING: INDEX FUTURES

Before we can proceed with the specific hedging examples in Chapters Three, Four, and Five, we need to determine what we are attempting to hedge and how that relates to our iron condor example. To hedge means to reduce risk. Hedging or reducing risk is synonymous with mitigating losses. As a result, we now need to create an objective set of rules that will define when we would exit the iron condor position for a loss.

In my most recent article *(Option Income Strategy Trade Filters)*, I dedicated a full-chapter to creating a comprehensive trade plan that described every possible entry and exit scenario for iron condors, and applied those objective rules historically to evaluate over 15,000 managed iron condor trades. Fortunately, we do not need a comprehensive trade plan to complete our practical hedging examples, but we will still need to identify the specific iron condor trade plan rules that would force us to exit the position for a loss.

## Iron Condor Exit Rules

As the price of the underlying security (SPX in our example) moves closer to the upper and lower loss regions of the iron condor payoff diagram, risk increases and return decreases. As a result, many option traders choose to exit credit spread trades (including iron condors) when the price of the underlying security reaches or "touches" the short strike price.

This is a very simple objective rule and it easy to apply. We will use this rule in our iron condor hedging examples. Figure 3.1 is another screen capture image of OptionVue's graphical analysis screen depicting our iron condor example at inception of the trade (intra-day on February 27, 2017). The format is the same as Figure 2.5, but the scale is different. As you can see in Figure 3.1, our iron condor used short put and short call positions with strike prices of $2,240 and $2,460 respectively. As a result, we would exit our iron condor position if the price of SPX dropped to $2,240 or if the price of SPX increased to $2,460.

In addition, we would exit the iron condor if the loss ever equaled 20% of the required capital. The required capital was $106,712, so we would exit the position if the loss ever equaled $21,342 (106,712 X 20%). These objective exit rules are designed to close the iron condor position before the risk-characteristics of the trade become unfavorable.

We obviously know the short strike prices, but we have to model the behavior of the iron condor position to determine the SPX price level that corresponds to a 20% loss. I manually added two perpendicular lines to OptionVue's graphical analysis screen in Figure 3.1. The two lines intersect the dotted T+0 line at the maximum 20% loss level. According to OptionVue's analysis, an instantaneous decline in SPX to $2,257.90 (-4.7%) would result in a loss equal to 20% of our required capital, which would trigger an exit.

## Unable to Exit

Ideally, we would like to use the 20% loss limit in the position sizing formulas outlined in Chapter One. However, as demonstrated in that chapter, in order to *guarantee* that our *actual* total capital at risk (TCAR) would not exceed our *desired* total capital at risk, we must ensure that we would actually be able to exit the trade if the loss equaled 20% of the position size ($21,342 = $106,712 X 20%).

In practice, the maximum loss amount must include slippage. Any unexpected slippage would result in a realized loss greater than our maximum specified risk threshold, which would put an excessive amount of our total capital at risk. As a result, it is critical to reduce slippage, but how do we do that, particularly when the options market is closed overnight? If the options market was closed, we would not be able to exit our option position as planned.

For example, if the price of the underlying security (SPX) was already approaching the maximum loss trigger price ($2,257.90), and the price of the underlying security (SPX) gapped down overnight, the value of the iron condor could plummet, resulting in a massive amount of slippage.

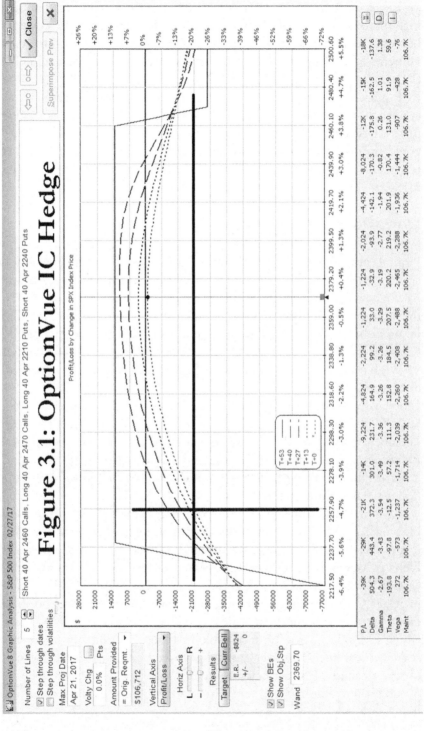

Figure 3.1: OptionVue IC Hedge

In this scenario, the actual loss could greatly exceed the specified maximum loss level of 20% or $21,342. Remember, iron condors become increasingly risky at the extremes, where they are very vulnerable to large discrete changes in price and implied volatility (IV).

But are those price and IV changes really discrete? Overnight gaps appear discrete when looking exclusively at the closing and opening prices. However, there are markets that are open almost 24/7 that we could use to hedge our option income strategies when exit rules are triggered outside of regular trading hours: the financial futures markets.

## Downside Futures Hedge

I briefly introduced the possibility of using futures to hedge option strategy exits in my last article (*Option Income Strategy Trade Filters*), but I will go much further in this chapter, including using OptionVue and the accompanying spreadsheet to identify the actual futures trades required to hedge the SPX iron condor position we created in Chapter Two.

We have already identified three SPX levels that would trigger an exit: short put strike at $2,240, maximum 20% loss level at $2,257.90, and short call strike at $2,460. The SPX price would obviously reach $2,257.90 before falling to $2,240, so our downside hedge would initially be placed at $2,257.90. We will use the interactive tool on the *FuturesHedge* tab (Figure 3.2) of the OSHRM.xlsm spreadsheet to calculate the number of futures contracts to buy or sell to hedge the downside iron condor exit.

As is the case throughout the spreadsheet, the cells with the solid blue background are for user inputs. In order to hedge the market risk at the target SPX price, we first need an estimate of the position Delta of our iron condor at that price level ($2,257.90). Fortunately, OptionVue calculates position Deltas at every SPX price level and provides these values on the graphical analysis screen. The position Delta for the T+0 line at the SPX exit price level ($2,257.90) is 372.3, which is shown in the bottom table in Figure 3.1 directly under the solid vertical line. The user can also move the vertical price "wand" to any desired SPX price level on the graphical analysis screen to observe the resulting P&L and Greek values. As I explained before, these values can be calculated for any of the T+ time lines.

The large positive position Delta (372.3) means that the value of our iron condor would *increase* by $372.3 for every one dollar *increase* in the price of SPX (after an instantaneous decline to $2,257.90). Even more important, our iron condor would *decrease* by $372.3 for every one dollar *decrease* in the price of SPX (from the same price level). You will recall that the initial position Delta was quite small, only 11.53. The increase in position Delta is a direct result of the significant decline in the SPX price. In other words, the value of our iron condor would decrease at a faster and faster rate as prices declined, due to the initial negative position Gamma (-3.33).

We enter the position Delta in Cell B4 of the *FuturesHedge* tab. The underlying security type is then entered in Cell B5 using a drop down box. This value is only used to modify the text in subsequent cells; it is not used in any calculations. In this case, the security type is "Index," indicating that the iron condor strategy was constructed with options on the S&P 500 *Index* (SPX).

The current price of the underlying security (SPX) is then entered in cell B6 ($2,366.40) and the current price of the corresponding hedging vehicle is entered in cell B7 ($2,365). In this case, the hedging vehicle is the E-mini S&P 500 futures contract (symbol ES), which has a multiplier of 50 (Cell B8). The price of the ES futures contract moves almost exactly dollar for dollar with the price of SPX. The only difference is due to the spread between the dividend yield of the S&P 500 index and the risk-free interest rate (the return on a cash investment).

However, the price of the underlying security would not always be comparable to the price of the futures hedging vehicle. For example, if we were hedging a comparable iron condor constructed with SPY (S&P 500 exchange traded fund) options, the price difference between the underlying security and the ES contract would be very large. Since the position Delta equals the linear change in the value of the position per one dollar increase in the price of the underlying security, the hedge calculation needs to account for this price difference - which it does. I did not include the SPY example here, because I did not want to complicate the hedging explanation. However, I encourage you to use your copy of the spreadsheet to calculate the required hedge for a SPY iron condor.

Returning to our SPX example in Figure 3.2, we entered the input values and the interactive tool calculated that we would need to sell seven ES futures (B9) contracts to hedge the position Delta risk of our iron condor, *but only if the price of SPX dropped to $2,257.90.* In addition, the resulting hedged position would still have a position Delta of 22.5, including the futures hedge. The reason is rounding. We can only trade an integer number of contracts.

| | Value | Description |
|---|---|---|
| | Copyright © 2017 Trading Insights, LLC. All Rights Reserved. | |
| | Figure 3.2: Hedging Option Strategy Exits | |
| | Value | Description |
| | 372.3 | Option Strategy: Position Delta* AT Desired Exit |
| | Index | Option Strategy: Underlying Security Type |
| | 2,366.400 | Option Strategy: Current Underlying Index Price |
| | 2,365.000 | Hedging Vehicle: Current Futures Price |
| | 50 | Futures: Multiplier (ES: 50, NQ: 20, TF: 100, ...) |
| | -7 | Hedge: Rounded Number of Futures Contracts |
| | 22.5 | Hedged Position: Remaining Position Delta* Risk |

Terms / Holidays / PositionSize / FuturesHedge

The purpose of the spreadsheet examples in this article is to explain how to use the spreadsheets, *not how to design or reconstruct the spreadsheets.* However, I will explain some of the calculations. The hedge calculation is particularly important, so I included the formula and calculation example below. All of the Delta values on the *FuturesHedge* tab are expressed in terms of changes in the price of the underlying security used to construct the option strategy, SPX in this example.

# Contracts = -Position Delta * (Underlying Price / Futures Price ) / Multiplier
# Contracts = - 372.3 * (2,366.4 / 2,365.0 ) / 50 = - 7.45, which is rounded to - 7.0
# Contracts = - 7 (Sell seven ES contracts)

Equivalent Hedge Delta = # Contracts * (Futures Price / Underlying Price) * Multiplier
Equivalent Hedge Delta = - 7 * (2,365 / 2,366.4) * 50
Equivalent Hedge Delta = - 349.8

Hedged Delta = Option Strategy Position Delta + Equivalent
   Hedge Delta
Hedged Delta = 372.3 + (- 349.8) = + 22.5 (B10)

## Actual Downside Hedge Transaction

The downside hedging calculation indicates that we should sell seven ES contracts, but what is the actual trade and when do we enter the order? Here is one possible order: a stop-limit order to sell seven E-mini S&P 500 futures contracts (ES) with a double-last trigger price of $2,258 and a limit price of $2,256. The order should be entered immediately after entering the iron condor position.

If two consecutive (double-last) ES trades are executed on the exchange at a price of $2,258 or lower, a limit order would automatically be placed to sell seven ES contracts at a price of $2,256 or better. I use the double-last trigger method to eliminate the possibility of a single erroneous trade triggering an unintended limit order on the exchange. The limit order price is placed below the trigger price to ensure the order is filled.

If you want to be even more confident of a fill, lower the limit price a little further. However, I personally do not use stop-market orders, which provide no price protection. To ensure my stop-limit orders are filled, I also enter text alerts on my broker platform for every trigger condition. This allows me to immediately log into my broker platform when a trigger condition is met, and adjust the limit price manually if necessary.

## Hedging Black-Swan Events

Why place the stop-limit order immediately after entering the iron condor? The futures hedge protects against conventional overnight gaps, which are not an immediate concern after entering the position. However, the black-swan events described in Chapter One could happen at any time, day or night. Would the futures stop-limit sell order protect us if a black swan type of event occurred when the futures market was open? There is no guarantee, but there is a good chance the order would be triggered and filled, which would substantially reduce our losses.

Consider a 9/11 type of event. These types of events often unfold over minutes or even hours. Even in today's world, there is typically no immediate widespread dissemination of *accurate* information regarding the event. Early conclusions are often erroneous and the true implications and scope of these types of events are not known in real time.

The most responsive traders would begin selling almost immediately as the news began to leak, putting downward pressure on prices. Market prices would drop rapidly and volatility would increase, but the ES contract is one of the most liquid instruments in the world, even during times of extreme volatility. As a result, ES slippage is exceptionally small. The hypothetical sell order would probably be filled almost instantaneously upon the price of the ES contract trading at $2,258 – provided the futures market was open at the time.

Unfortunately, there is no guarantee that the futures market would be open at the time of the event. The ES contract begins trading on Sunday evening and the market remains open approximately 23 hours per day until the following Friday evening. The exchange is then closed from Friday evening until Sunday evening.

As a result, there is a 71% (5/7) probability that the futures exchange would be open at the time of a hypothetical black-swan event. In addition, there is always the chance a senior Government official could decide to close the exchanges (before our futures hedge was executed) in response to a black-swan event, which happened on 9/11.

As a result, futures hedges are not 100% reliable. So why place the order if there is no guarantee it would be filled? Because it's *free*. If the futures order was never filled, there would be no cost. If it was filled, then our option strategy risk and potential losses would be dramatically reduced. It is a free option, one that every option trader should use religiously. How do we protect our option positions against excessive losses in the event that our protective futures order are *not filled*? That will be addressed in Chapters Four and Five, which also have their own dedicated spreadsheet tools.

## Futures Hedge Results

Let's review a specific hedging scenario assuming the futures stop-limit sell order *was filled* at the SPX maximum loss trigger price of $2,258 from our earlier example. I used OptionVue to model the change in the value of our SPX iron condor position in an extreme hypothetical scenario: a 10% overnight decline in the price of SPX, which occurred immediately after the trade was originated on February 27, 2017. The vertical "wand" is positioned at the SPX price of $2,129 in Figure 3.3, which corresponds to a decline of 10% from the SPX price of $2,366 at the inception of the trade. The table at the bottom of OptionVue's graphical analysis screen in Figure 3.3 shows a loss of $86K, but the OptionVue software also provides a more accurate loss of $85,620 on the unhedged iron condor position.

Figure 3.4 summarizes the results of the short seven contract ES futures hedge we calculated earlier using the *FuturesHedge* tab (Figure 3.2) of the spreadsheet. In the down 10% scenario, the gains in the E-mini short position would have offset $45,124 of the $85,620 iron condor overnight loss. The loss on the hedged position (including futures slippage and commissions) would have been $40,611 instead of $85,620. The $0.25 round-trip bid-ask spread on seven ES contracts, plus commissions of $2 per futures contract, would have only cost an additional $116. Not a bad investment: $116 to save $45,009.

The unhedged loss on required capital would have been 80.2% (Figure 3.4), far in excess of our 20% maximum projected loss. The loss on the hedged position (including the short ES futures position) would have been 38.1%, which would still have significantly exceeded our 20% desired maximum loss.

Why would the hedged position lose 38.1%, when the futures hedge was successfully executed at the maximum loss trigger price on the SPX? The first reason is relatively easy. The hedging calculations that followed Figure 3.2 demonstrated that the hedge actually required us to sell 7.45 ES contracts, not seven ES contracts. As a result, even after executing the seven contract hedge, the position Delta was still positive 22.5, not zero. A position Delta of 22.5 on a $100K position is not large, but it is significant when SPX prices decline 10% overnight.

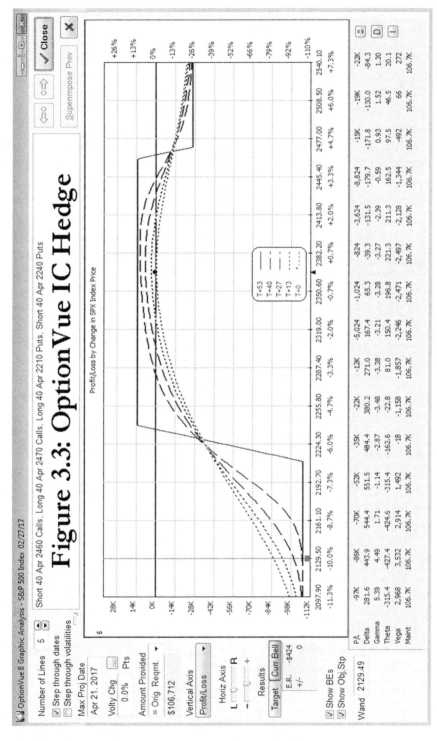

Figure 3.3: OptionVue IC Hedge

| Figure 3.4: E-mini S&P 500 (ES) Futures Hedge (- 7 Contracts) | | |
|---|---|---|
| Position | Position Delta @ SPX $2,258 | Overnight Gain: SPX $2,129 (-10%) |
| Unhedged Iron Condor | 372.3 | -85,620 |
| Sell 7 E-mini S&P 500 Futures (ES) | -349.8 | 45,124 |
| Hedge Transaction Cost | N/A | -116 |
| Hedged Position | 22.5 | -40,611 |
| Hedge Savings | N/A | 45,009 |
| Hedged Return on Required Capital | N/A | -38.1% |
| Unhedged Return on Required Capital | N/A | -80.2% |

Given that the actual hedge calculation was near the midpoint between seven and eight ES contracts, I also calculated the results of the futures hedge using eight ES contracts (Figure 3.5). In the down 10% scenario, the gains in the eight contract E-mini short position would have offset $51,574 of the $85,620 iron condor overnight loss. The loss on the hedged position (including futures slippage and commissions) would have been $34,178 instead of $85,620. The futures transaction costs would have added an additional $132, but would have saved $51,442.

The loss on the hedged position (including the short eight contract ES futures position) would have been 32.0%, which would have been better than 38.1%, but would still have exceeded our 20% desired maximum loss. So why couldn't we limit our losses to 20% with a futures hedge implemented at the maximum loss trigger price? Take a minute to consider the question.

| Figure 3.5: E-mini S&P 500 (ES) Futures Hedge (- 8 Contracts) | | |
|---|---|---|
| Position | Position Delta @ SPX $2,258 | Overnight Gain: SPX $2,129 (-10%) |
| Unhedged Iron Condor | 372.3 | -85,620 |
| Sell 8 E-mini S&P 500 Futures (ES) | -399.8 | 51,574 |
| Hedge Transaction Cost | N/A | -132 |
| Hedged Position | -27.5 | -34,178 |
| Hedge Savings | N/A | 51,442 |
| Hedged Return on Required Capital | N/A | -32.0% |
| Unhedged Return on Required Capital | N/A | -80.2% |

The answer is negative Gamma. If you look back at OptionVue's graphical analysis screen in Figure 3.1, you will discover that the position Gamma would have been negative 3.54 at the SPX maximum loss trigger price ($2,257.90). That was even worse (more negative) than the position Gamma at the inception of the trade (-3.33). The negative Gamma would have caused Delta to continue to increase as the SPX price plunged further. This would have forced the iron condor losses to accumulate at a faster and faster rate.

As you can see in Figure 3.1, the position Delta would have continued to increase at prices below the SPX trigger/hedge point ($2,257.90). When the hedge was implemented, the position Delta would have been +372.3. At the SPX price of $2,217.5, the position Delta would have jumped to +504.3, which would have required a short position of *ten* ES contracts, not *seven*. In other words, changes in the ES futures price are a *linear* function (*zero Gamma*) of the change in SPX, and iron condor price changes are a *non-linear* function (*negative Gamma*) of the change in SPX.

If you wanted to further mitigate your potential catastrophic losses, you could use OptionVue's graphical analysis screen to estimate the position Deltas at price levels below the initial hedge level. These values could then be used in conjunction with the *FuturesHedge* tools (shown in Figure 3.2) to identify trigger-price levels for additional stop-limit orders to sell incremental ES contracts as needed to dynamically hedge the iron condor position.

## Unwinding the Hedge

As the hedge results in Figures 3.4 and 3.5 demonstrate, the futures hedge does not eliminate all risk. It only hedges a portion of the position Delta risk at a specified price level. It does not eliminate Gamma risk or Vega risk. We would still need to exit the iron condor position and unwind the hedge to eliminate all remaining risk.

In the preceding scenario, an overnight price decline of 10% in the SPX would create havoc in the options market when options trading resumed the next day. Depending on the reason for the brutal price decline, option liquidity could be severely limited for an extended period. Even worse, the market could be closed, as it was on 9/11.

If we were unhedged, our losses would already be excessive and we would still be exposed to even greater losses. Every other *unhedged* option income trader would also be hemorrhaging losses and everyone would be scrambling for the exits at the same time. Can you imagine the prices the *unhedged* traders would need to pay to buy back their short Gamma positions? You could certainly forget about mid-market execution. Market makers would charge exorbitant prices for assuming the *unhedged* traders' cumulative position risk in such a highly volatile environment. It is painful to even consider this scenario. The only good news is that the *hedged* traders would have a lot less competition going forward.

To appreciate the unique market environment, it was important to paint that rather vivid picture. Now let's get back to unwinding our hedged position. Unlike all of the unhedged traders, our losses would still be manageable. If we dynamically hedged our negative Gamma position with futures, our losses would be even lower. And we would still be Delta-hedged the next morning. In other words, we would have the luxury of time in unwinding our position.

The ideal way to exit the hedged position is to enter a limit order to buy back the iron condor position at a *reasonable* price, not at the *extortionate* prices paid by the unhedged traders. Immediately after the option limit order is filled, we would place a limit order to buy back the short ES futures contracts. Due to the exceptional liquidity in the ES futures market, the futures order would be filled almost instantaneously. That is why we execute the options order first, to minimize the potentially massive slippage in the options market, which is especially important in highly volatile environments.

## Intra-Day Futures Hedge

If we entered the futures stop-limit order immediately after entering the iron condor trade, there would be no reason to expect the futures hedge to be executed exclusively during the overnight trading session. It could also be triggered and executed during the regular daily trading hours for both options and futures.

This would be beneficial if the futures hedge was triggered when we were out for a quick lunch. However, even if we were sitting in front of our trading platform when an exit rule was triggered, the immediate futures Delta-hedge would still provide some benefit. It would give us time to work the limit order and exit the iron condor position at the best possible price level, as close as possible to mid-market execution. Futures transaction costs are insignificant compared to the slippage costs of a rushed iron condor exit.

## Adjusting the Downside Hedge

Earlier in this chapter we identified the exit rules for our iron condor. We would exit if the SPX price touched the strike price of the short put ($2,240) or the short call ($2,460). These exit prices are obviously static and would not change. In addition, we would also exit the iron condor if the loss ever equaled 20% of the required capital. The required capital was $106,712, so we would exit the position if the loss ever equaled $21,342 ($106,712 X 20%).

As explained earlier, we had to model the behavior of the iron condor position to determine the SPX price level that corresponded to a 20% loss. The two perpendicular lines in Figure 3.1 intersect the dotted T+0 line at the maximum 20% loss level. According to OptionVue's analysis, an instantaneous decline in SPX to $2,257.90 (-4.7%) would result in a loss equal to 20% of our required capital, which would trigger an exit. We used the $2,257.90 SPX trigger price value earlier in our hedging examples.

However, this trigger price would not be constant. It would respond to changes in several different variables: the price of the underlying security, the time remaining until expiration, the implied volatility, and the volatility skews. These changes would require us to adjust our downside futures hedge.

One way to see this effect is to look back at Figure 3.1. The horizontal maximum loss line intersects the T+0 line at an SPX price of $2,257.90, but it intersects the T+13, T+27, T+40, and T+53 lines at successively lower SPX price levels. In other words, successively lower SPX prices would be required to generate the same 20% loss over longer holding periods. Why? Because the additional income from positive Theta would offset the adverse effects of negative Gamma, which would allow us to withstand lower SPX prices over longer holding periods.

While the modeling is complex, adjusting the futures hedge is quick and easy – with the right tools. After initiating the iron condor trade, we would enter the trade in OptionVue or a similar analytical platform. Once the trade is entered, OptionVue will automatically recalculate the scenario Greeks and profit and loss values on the graphical analysis screen.

Simply identify the point where the maximum loss line intersects the T+0 line (as shown in Figure 3.1) and enter the resulting position Delta in the *FuturesHedge* tab (Cell B4 in Figure 3.2), which will recalculate the required number of futures contracts (Cell B9 in Figure 3.2). Modify the futures order prices and/or the number of futures contracts as needed using your broker's platform. It should take no longer than a few minutes.

## Upside Futures Hedge

We have already identified the SPX price level that would trigger an exit on the upside: the short call strike price at $2,460. We will again use the interactive tool on the *FuturesHedge* tab (Figure 3.6) of the OSHRM.xlsm spreadsheet to calculate the number of futures contracts to buy or sell to hedge the upside iron condor exit.

In order to hedge the market risk at the target SPX price, we first need an estimate of the position Delta of our iron condor at that SPX exit price level ($2,460). As explained earlier, OptionVue calculates position Deltas at every SPX price level and provides these values on the graphical analysis screen (Figure 3.1). The position Delta for the T+0 line at the $2,460 SPX price level is negative 175.8, which is shown in the bottom table in Figure 3.1 directly under the $2,460 (+3.8%) price level. Note that we do not need to be concerned about the 20% maximum loss level on the upside, because our iron condor would never lose more than 20% of our required capital when SPX prices rise (see Figure 3.1).

The negative position Delta (-175.8) means that the value of our iron condor would *decrease* by $175.8 for every one dollar *increase* in the price of SPX (after an instantaneous increase to $2,460). We enter the position negative 175.8 position Delta in Cell B4 of the *FuturesHedge* tab (Figure 3.6). The underlying security type is then entered in Cell B5 using a drop-down box. As was the case in the downside hedge, the security type is "Index," indicating that the iron condor strategy was constructed with options on the S&P 500 *Index* (SPX).

The current price of the underlying security (SPX) is then entered in cell B6 ($2,366.40) and the current price of the corresponding hedging vehicle is entered in cell B7 ($2,365). The hedging vehicle is again the E-mini S&P 500 futures contracts (symbol ES), which has a multiplier of 50 (Cell B8).

For the upside hedge in Figure 3.6, we entered the input values and the interactive tool calculated that we would need to *buy* four ES futures contracts (B9) to hedge the negative position Delta risk of our iron condor, *but only if the price of SPX increased to $2,460.* The resulting hedged position would still have a position Delta of +24.1, including the hedge. Again, the reason is rounding. We can only trade an integer number of futures contracts.

| |  |  |
|---|---|---|
| 1 | Copyright © 2017 Trading Insights, LLC. All Rights Reserved. | |
| 2 | Figure 3.6: Hedging Option Strategy Exits | |
| 3 | Value | Description |
| 4 | -175.8 | Option Strategy: Position Delta* AT Desired Exit |
| 5 | Index | Option Strategy: Underlying Security Type |
| 6 | 2,366.400 | Option Strategy: Current Underlying Index Price |
| 7 | 2,365.000 | Hedging Vehicle: Current Futures Price |
| 8 | 50 | Futures: Multiplier (ES: 50, NQ: 20, TF: 100, ...) |
| 9 | 4 | Hedge: Rounded Number of Futures Contracts |
| 10 | 24.1 | Hedged Position: Remaining Position Delta* Risk |

**# Contracts = - Position Delta * (Underlying Price / Futures Price ) / Multiplier**
**# Contracts = - (- 175.8) * (2,366.4 / 2,365.0 ) / 50 = 3.52, which is rounded to 4.0**
**# Contracts = + 4 (Buy four ES contracts)**

**Equivalent Hedge Delta = # Contracts * (Futures Price / Underlying Price) * Multiplier**
**Equivalent Hedge Delta = 4 * (2,365 / 2,366.4) * 50**
**Equivalent Hedge Delta = 199.9**

**Hedged Delta = Option Strategy Position Delta + Equivalent Hedge Delta**
**Hedged Delta = -175.8 + 199.9) = + 24.1 (B10)**

## Actual Upside Hedge Transaction

The upside hedging calculation indicates that we should buy four ES contracts. Here is an example of the order: a stop-limit order to buy four E-mini S&P 500 futures contracts (ES) with a double-last trigger price of $2,460 and a limit price of $2,462. The order should be entered immediately after entering the iron condor position.

If two consecutive (double-last) ES trades are executed on the exchange at a price of $2,460 or higher, a limit order would automatically be placed to buy four ES contracts at a price of $2,462 or better. As I explained before, to ensure my stop-limit orders are filled, I also enter text alerts on my broker platform for every trigger condition. This allows me to immediately log into my broker platform when a trigger condition is met, and adjust the limit price manually if necessary.

Since the upside and downside futures hedges would never both be executed, the trades can be entered as a group trade, where execution of the one order would automatically cancel the other order. If the exchange prohibits entering simultaneous stop-buy and stop-sell orders on the same futures contract, you should still be able to create two separate conditional orders on your broker platform. Instead of being monitored on the exchange, the order conditions would be monitored automatically by your broker and the limit orders would be submitted to the exchange immediately if the trigger conditions were satisfied.

Our example iron condor used SPX options, but the hedging techniques introduced in this chapter are applicable to many different types of instruments. Similar hedges can be executed using futures on the RUT and NDX indices and the accompanying spreadsheet can accommodate any underlying security.

## Conclusion

It takes time to get exit orders filled on iron condors when markets are volatile; futures hedges remove time pressure by instantaneously reducing market risk, even when options markets are closed. Using futures to hedge option income strategy exits substantially reduces both transaction costs and potential losses.

Failing to use futures to hedge market risk when exit rules are triggered is one of the most frequent and significant oversights made by option income strategy traders. Mastering this technique could save you tens of thousands of dollars and greatly reduce your risk.

However, there is no guarantee that our futures hedge orders will always be executed, especially when discrete black-swan events occur. As a result, we need a second, more reliable hedging approach to manage and mitigate our catastrophic event risk. Chapters Four and Five will present two alternative hedging instruments; both will include detailed spreadsheet examples.

# 4 - HEDGING: VIX CALL OPTIONS

The goal of this chapter is to introduce an analytical framework and the corresponding spreadsheet tools that will allow us to identify the most efficient *VIX call option hedge* to mitigate the risk of random catastrophic events. Hedges using *put options on the underlying security* (SPX) will be examined in Chapter Five. Both of these chapters will assume that the futures hedge transactions explained in Chapter Three were *not executed* and our options strategy was still exposed to 100% losses.

Both types of market-specific hedge solutions (call and put) will be derived from real-time market prices and from user-specific market scenarios. Furthermore, the analytical frameworks and spreadsheet tools for the VIX call and underlying put hedges are very similar, and the cost of VIX call and underlying put hedges will be directly comparable. This will allow us to use the spreadsheet tools to identify the most efficient hedge solution in any market environment, for any user scenario.

I will begin with a higher-level conceptual overview of the VIX index and related instruments, which will also explain a number of the terms and concepts used throughout this chapter. The purpose of this overview is to provide the requisite foundation before we delve into the operational mechanics of the spreadsheet tools and the resulting hedging transactions.

## The VIX Index

The hedging technique explained in this chapter will require purchasing deep out-of-the money (OTM) call options on the VIX index. As a result, a basic understanding of the VIX index is essential.

The VIX index is a volatility index derived from the prices and implied volatilities of options on the S&P 500 index (SPX). The options used to derive the VIX index are out-of-the money (OTM) SPX calls and puts with expiration dates that bracket the VIX index's constant 30-day time-to-expiration. For a more complete description of the CBOE VIX index, see the CBOE's VIX Index white paper, which can be found at https://www.cboe.com/micro/vix/vixwhite.pdf.

The VIX index is expressed in units of annualized implied volatility. For example, a VIX index value of 17.76 would equate to an annualized implied volatility of 17.76%. Before using the VIX as a hedging vehicle, it is essential to understand how the VIX index has behaved historically and how it responds to changing market conditions.

Fortunately, the CBOE provides free historical data on the VIX index from 1/2/1990 through the present. I used this data to calculate the VIX Index percentile ranks, which are summarized in Figure 4.0. From 1990 to March 2017 the VIX index ranged from a low of 9.31 to a high of 80.86. The median value was 17.76, which represents the midpoint of the dataset. Exactly 50% of the end-of-day VIX index observations were above 17.76 and 50% were below. If you have not studied the VIX index, I encourage you to use this table regularly to provide a historical context for current VIX index values.

As you can see from the data, the VIX index is skewed heavily to the upside. In other words, the difference between the 100th percentile (80.86) and the 50th percentile (17.76) is much larger than the difference between the 50th percentile (17.76) and the 0th percentile (9.31). The *average* VIX index value from 1990 to March 2017 was 19.63, which was significantly larger than the *median* value of 17.76. This difference is also indicative of a positively skewed distribution.

Understanding the historical distribution of the VIX index data is important, but there is another characteristic that is even more important to understand from a hedging perspective: how the VIX index responds to price changes in the S&P 500 index (SPX).

| Figure 4.0: VIX Index Percentile (1990 - 3/2017) ||
| Percentile Rank | VIX Index |
| --- | --- |
| 100% | 80.86 |
| 98% | 42.13 |
| 95% | 33.61 |
| 90% | 28.90 |
| 80% | 24.39 |
| 70% | 21.76 |
| 60% | 19.72 |
| 50% | 17.76 |
| 40% | 16.17 |
| 30% | 14.67 |
| 20% | 13.31 |
| 10% | 12.14 |
| 5% | 11.51 |
| 2% | 11.02 |
| 0% | 9.31 |

When the price of SPX increases, the implied volatilities of SPX options decline, which means that the VIX index also declines. Conversely, when the price of SPX declines, the implied volatilities of SPX options increase, which means that the VIX index also increases. This should be somewhat intuitive. In the equity market, stock prices fall faster than they rise. This increased volatility makes options more valuable, which translates to higher implied volatilities, and higher VIX values.

We need to quantify the relationship between VIX and SPX before we can create reliable VIX hedging solutions. To do so, I solved for the slope ($\beta$ or Beta) term in the following linear regression, which used daily closing prices from 2004 to February 2017:

$$\text{VIX}_T - \text{VIX}_{T-1} = \beta * \text{LN} (\text{SPX}_T/\text{SPX}_{T-1}) + \varepsilon$$

**$VIX_T$: VIX Index Time T**
**$VIX_{T-1}$ : VIX Index Time T-1 (one day earlier)**

**$\beta$: Beta or slope coefficient**
**LN: Natural Log Function**
**$\epsilon$: error term**

**$SPX_T$: SPX Price Time T**
**$SPX_{T-1}$: SPX Price Time T-1 (one day earlier)**

The Beta coefficient was -124.001 and the results of the linear regression were highly significant. The t-statistic of the Beta term was -88.06 and the R-Square value of the regression was 0.705, which indicates that the regression explained 70.5% of the variation in the VIX index. The correlation between the daily change in the VIX index (dependent variable) and the natural log of the daily SPX return (independent variable) was -0.840. This was an extremely strong negative correlation. Negative 1.0 signifies a perfect negative correlation.

The following actual two SPX and VIX daily examples from 2008 may provide additional insight into the practical value of the regression equation.

**$VIX_T - VIX_{T-1} = \beta * LN (SPX_T/SPX_{T-1}) + \epsilon$**

**09/29/2008: 46.72 − 34.74 = 124.001 * LN (1106.42/1213.27) + $\epsilon$**
**09/29/2008: 11.98 = - 124.001 * LN (0.91193) + $\epsilon$**
**09/29/2008: 11.98 = - 124.001 * - 0.09219 + $\epsilon$**
**09/29/2008: 11.98 = 11.43 + $\epsilon$**
**09/29/2008: $\epsilon$ (error) = 0.55**

**$VIX_T - VIX_{T-1} = \beta * \ln (SPX_T/SPX_{T-1}) + \epsilon$**

**10/28/2008: 66.96 − 80.06 = 124.001 * LN (940.51/848.92) + $\epsilon$**
**10/28/2008: - 13.10 = - 124.001 * LN (1.10789) + $\epsilon$**
**10/28/2008: - 13.10 = - 124.001 * 0.10246 + $\epsilon$**
**10/28/2008: - 13.10 = - 12.70 + $\epsilon$**
**10/28/2008: $\epsilon$ (error) = - 0.40**

The preceding examples from the Great Recession in 2008 represent two of the most extreme daily changes in the SPX and in the VIX index in the past 27 years. The estimated VIX changes were very accurate, even in this extreme market environment.

The very strong negative correlation between SPX prices and the VIX index makes the VIX index a very attractive hedging vehicle. Unfortunately, the VIX index is not investible. In other words, it is not possible to buy or sell the VIX index directly. As a result, we will need to explore derivatives of the VIX index: VIX futures and VIX options.

## VIX Futures

Since we will be using VIX call options to hedge random catastrophic events, it might seem strange to review VIX futures as well. However, VIX *option* prices are derived from expected future VIX values and our best source of these values is the VIX futures market. In order to understand how VIX options are priced, it is vital to understand the behavior of VIX futures.

Since the VIX index is not investible or deliverable, VIX futures are cash settled using a special opening quotation of the VIX index. The VIX futures contract multiplier is 1000. Monthly VIX futures contracts expire on the Wednesday that is 30 days prior to the expiration date of the subsequent month's SPX monthly option contracts. Weekly VIX futures contracts were introduced more recently and they also expire on Wednesdays. For more information on the CBOE VIX (VX) Futures, see the CBOE's education site: http://cfe.cboe.com/education/vixprimer/basics.aspx

## VIX Futures Term Structure

At any given time, there are a number of different VIX futures contracts outstanding, each with a different settlement or expiration date. The real-time prices of the VIX futures contracts represent the market's best collective estimates of the values of the VIX index on those future dates.

Figure 4.1 is a graph of the VIX futures term structure on four different dates. The expiration months are shown on the horizontal axis. Zero represents the actual VIX index; one represents the first monthly futures contract, two represents the second monthly futures contract, and so on. The VIX futures prices are shown on the vertical axis. Each line represents the collection of monthly VIX futures prices (the VIX term structure) on a given date.

The top line represents an extreme fear or panic environment during a period of extraordinary volatility (10/17/2008). For those of you who were trading in 2008, you will remember this period well. Moving down the chart, the next VIX term structure example occurred only two weeks earlier (10/3/2008). Volatility was unusually high and fear was still evident, but panic had not yet set in.

The next VIX term structure example (1/29/2016) was during a period of elevated risk with widespread uncertainty about the direction of the economy and the market. The bottom line represents a period of complacency with relatively low volatility (11/21/2013).

I will review this chart in detail, but first I wanted to challenge you to draw your own conclusions. What do you notice about the shape of the VIX term structure in the four different environments? Why would those particular shapes exist in each environment? What do the respective shapes say about the market's future volatility expectations?

What do you notice about the relative volatility of VIX futures prices as a function of the time-to-expiration? What are the trading and hedging implications?

The slopes of the four VIX futures term structures in Figure 4.1 are very different. The term structure on 10/17/2008 (top line) began with a VIX index value of 67.65 and then sloped downward sharply. Why? Because the initial VIX index value (67.65) was so extreme. It was in the 99.8th percentile. Only 0.2% of the VIX index observations in the past 27 years exceeded 67.65. As a result, it is not surprising that the market collectively expected the VIX index to decline (revert back toward the mean) going forward.

The same phenomenon was evident on 10/3/2008. The VIX index value was not quite as extreme, but was still in the 98.5th percentile. As a result, the VIX futures term structure still had a downward slope.

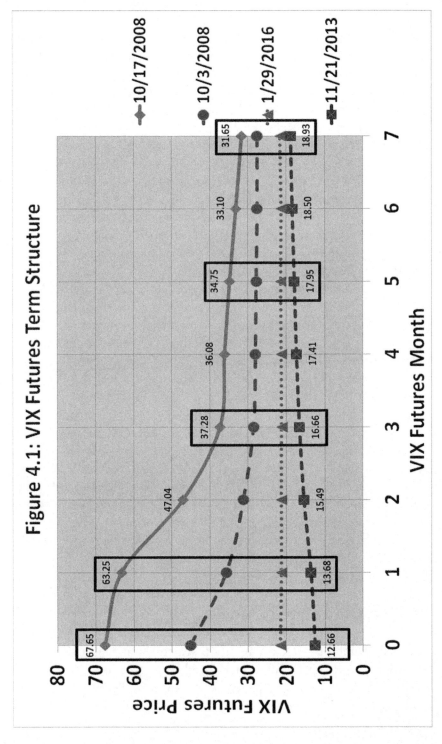

Figure 4.1: VIX Futures Term Structure

There is another important observation about high volatility environments that many traders miss. In order for implied volatility and the VIX index to *remain* high after a discrete shock, realized or actual volatility must also remain high. In other words, if the market declined by 20% overnight, implied volatility and the VIX index would definitely spike. Based on our regression equation, the VIX would probably increase by over 22 points.

Continuing with this hypothetical scenario, let's assume the VIX index jumped from 58.86 to its 27-year high of 80.86. In order for the VIX index to remain at 80.86, *daily volatility would need to exceed 5%, and the market would probably need to decline even further.* Even in that scenario, the VIX futures term structure would be downward sloping. Once the actual daily market volatility dropped below 5% (80.86 / ((252)^0.5)) and the market began to stabilize, implied volatilities would drop sharply, as would the VIX index.

The VIX term structure on 1/29/2016 was almost perfectly flat and the VIX values were only slightly above the average VIX value in the past 27 years. The flat term structure suggests that there was no general consensus for a significant increase or decrease in the VIX index. Instead, VIX futures prices reflected the increased level of uncertainty regarding the direction of the market and the economy that prevailed in early 2016.

Finally, the VIX futures prices on 11/21/2013 (bottom line) reflected the "normal" upward-sloping shape of the VIX term structure. The VIX index was 12.66, which was only in the 14th percentile. In other words, 86% of the VIX observations in the past 27 years exceeded 12.66. As a result, it is not surprising that the market collectively expected the VIX index to increase going forward, which is consistent with the upward-sloping curve.

The key observation is that volatility, the VIX index, and the VIX futures term structure are all mean-reverting. This has important implications for the relative volatility of VIX futures contracts.

## VIX Futures Volatility Model

Let's reexamine the VIX futures term structures in Figure 4.1. In the four examples, the VIX index fluctuated between a low of 12.66 and a high of 67.65, which equates to a range of 54.99 points. The resulting ranges of the one, three, five, and seven month VIX futures contracts were 49.57 (63.25 - 13.68), 20.62 (37.28 − 16.66), 16.80 (34.75 − 17.95), and 12.72 (31.65 − 18.93), respectively. The relative futures volatility dropped sharply (and non-linearly) as a function of the number of months remaining until contract expiration. The decline in relative volatility is a direct result of mean-reversion, which is common to other financial term structures, including the term structure of interest rates, although the underlying mathematics are different.

What are the trading and hedging implications of the volatility differences across the VIX futures term structure? Since we will be using VIX call options to hedge random catastrophic events, and VIX *options* prices are derived from VIX futures prices, we will need to incorporate a more precise VIX futures volatility model into our hedging framework.

In an effort to exploit inefficiencies in VIX futures prices, I began developing a proprietary hedged VIX futures trading strategy several months ago. The strategy was complex and required separate but integrated risk, valuation, forecasting, and optimization models. After completing and implementing the new VIX futures trading strategy, I immediately recognized that the VIX futures risk model component could be used to construct VIX call hedge solutions that accurately modeled the relative volatility differences across the entire term structure of volatilities.

Incorporating realistic relative volatility differences is a critical step in creating realistic hedge solutions, one that even professional option traders often overlook. If a trader mistakenly assumed that the term structure of expected volatilities moved in a parallel fashion, it would result in grossly inaccurate hedge solutions that offered little or no protection against random catastrophic events.

I used the entire historical data set for all monthly VIX futures contracts in developing and estimating the VIX futures risk model. This included data on over 155 separate futures contracts from 2004 to 2017. The resulting VIX futures risk model is very simple conceptually. The following non-linear model estimates the daily percentage change in the VIX futures price for a given daily change in the VIX index. In other words, the model solves for the expected change in the price of a VIX futures contract, expressed as a percentage of the change in the VIX index.

The only required input variable is the number of *trade days remaining until expiration* (TDTE) of the VIX futures contract. In addition, there are three parameters or constants (M, B, and C) that were estimated using the entire daily history of VIX futures prices. I used the Generalized Reduced Gradient (GRG) non-linear optimization algorithm to solve for the model coefficients (M, B, and C) that minimized the model errors in the 13 years of daily historical data.

**M = - 0.144269504088896**
**B = - 0.889848726630335**
**C = - 12.3388270923591**

**VIX Futures Relative Price Change =**

**[(1.0 + M * LN(TDTE)) + (1.0 + B * (1 - Exp(C * (TDTE / 252))))]/2**

**LN: Natural Log Function**
**EXP: e (or 2.71828) raised to the power**
**TDTE: Trade days till expiration**

The following example assumes a VIX futures contract with 41 trade days remaining until expiration (approximately two months).

**VIX Futures Relative Price Change =**

**[(1.0 + M * LN(TDTE)) + (1.0 + B * (1 - Exp(C * (TDTE / 252))))]/2**

**[(1.0 + M * LN(41)) + (1.0 + B * (1 - Exp(C * (41 / 252))))]/2**

**[(0.4642) + (0.2297)]/2 = 0.3470 = 34.70%**

The example indicates that the price of a VIX futures contract with 41 trade days remaining until expiration would change by 34.70% of the change in the VIX index. If the VIX index increased by 5.0 points, we would expect the 41 trade-day VIX futures contract to increase by 1.74 dollars (5.0 X 34.70%). If the VIX index decreased by 2.0 points, we would expect the 41 trade-day VIX futures contract to decrease by 0.70 dollars (-2 X 34.70%).

The graph in Figure 4.2 shows the relative volatility of the VIX futures term structure, which was derived using the preceding VIX futures risk model. Several futures contracts with a range of expiration dates are included in the graph to provide additional insight into the relative volatility of the entire term structure of expected volatilities.

## VIX Options

Now that we have reviewed the VIX index and VIX futures, we can begin to explore the vehicle that we will use to construct catastrophic risk hedges in the remainder of this chapter: VIX options. VIX options have several features that are unique from equity and index options. The first and most important difference is that VIX option prices are derived from the expected future value of the VIX index. As explained earlier in this chapter, VIX futures prices are real-time proxies for the market's best collective estimates of the values of the VIX index in the future.

The VIX futures price can be used to represent the underlying price of the VIX index in option valuation and risk models. In other words, VIX futures prices define the at-the-money level for all VIX options. The January VIX futures price defines the at-the-money level for VIX options expiring in January; the same relationship applies to VIX options expiring in February, March, April, and all other months.

The forward pricing relationship is much simpler in equities. Except for specific stocks that are difficult to borrow (sell short), the expected future price of stocks and equity indices is a known function of the risk-free interest rate and the dividend yield of the underlying stock. The relationship between the current price of a stock or equity index and its forward price is subject to arbitrage, which forces the forward price to follow a known predictable path.

The opposite is true for VIX futures and VIX options. VIX futures prices represent the best estimate of future VIX index levels, but it is not possible to arbitrage this relationship, because the VIX index is not investable. As a result, changes in VIX futures prices do not follow a known predictable path. That is the reason that we need a VIX futures risk model, to accurately price VIX options.

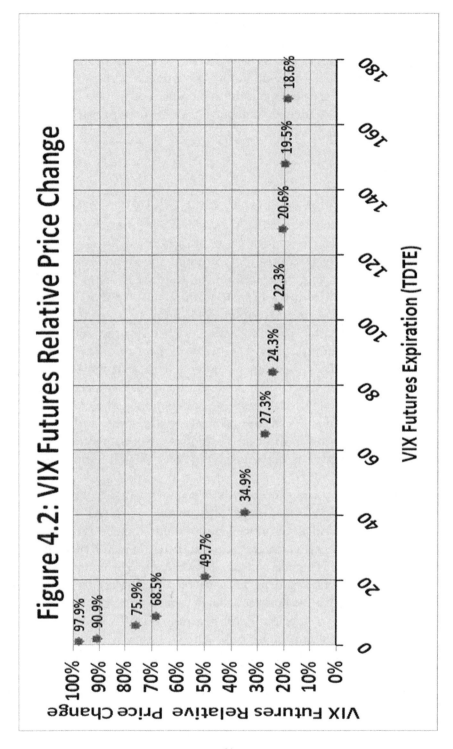

Figure 4.2: VIX Futures Relative Price Change

VIX options and futures are cash-settled on Wednesdays, based on a special opening quotation. Since the VIX index is not deliverable, cash-settlement is required. It is not possible to take "physical" delivery of the VIX index.

The other important characteristic of the VIX index is that it is highly volatile. Even if the VIX index was at the very low level of 12, it could easily jump to 16 the same day, which would represent an increase of 33.3%. The resulting annualized realized volatility would be approximately 529%.

Depending on the pricing model, implied volatilities of VIX options regularly exceed 100%, especially for near-term options. Why did I highlight near-term VIX options? Because the volatility of near-term VIX futures contracts is much higher than the volatility of long-term VIX futures contracts. This relationship was illustrated in Figure 4.2. The relative volatility differences in VIX futures contracts directly influence the prices of VIX options, which will be critically important when constructing hedge solutions with VIX options.

## VIX Call Hedge Spreadsheet Overview

As explained earlier, the purpose of the spreadsheet examples in this article is to explain how to *use* the spreadsheets, *not how to design or reconstruct the spreadsheets*. In addition, I will not attempt to explain every intermediate cell calculation. This is particularly true of the *VIXCallHedge* spreadsheet example in this chapter and the *EQPutHedge* spreadsheet example in the next chapter, both of which require some complex computations. However, I will explain the calculations and spreadsheet functions (in general terms) when necessary for additional clarity or comprehension.

This section will provide a brief overview of the *VIXCallHedge* spreadsheet, which should make it easier to understand the steps required to use the spreadsheet in practice, which we will cover in detail in the following sections. The objective of the *VIXCallHedge* spreadsheet is to calculate the total dollar cost of the hedge per trade-day for a list of weekly and monthly VIX call options. These values can then be compared for all option candidates to identify the most cost-efficient hedging solution.

In addition, the total cost-per-day of maintaining the catastrophic risk hedge should be compared to the expected and/or historical profit-per-trade of the specific option strategy. This will determine the long-term viability of the option strategy *after* managing the risk of a black-swan event.

There are six principal components of the *VIXCallHedge* spreadsheet:

1. Hedge Objective,
2. Catastrophic Risk Event,
3. Market Data,
4. Option Valuation,
5. Hedge Solution, and
6. Scenario Analysis

We will review each of these components in detail in the following sections, including an explanation of the steps required to use the spreadsheet and what those steps accomplish. As you work through the remainder of this chapter, always remember the goal of the *VIXCallHedge* spreadsheet: to calculate and find the lowest-cost VIX call option hedging solution. Consider how each step and piece of information helps us reach that goal.

The spreadsheet has a number of input, intermediate, and output values. I designed the spreadsheet so that all of the required cells can be displayed simultaneously on a single computer monitor. Unfortunately, a single image of the entire *VIXCallHedge* spreadsheet tab would not be readable in a book.

As a result, I was forced to create partial images of the *VIXCallHedge* spreadsheet tab in this publication. I will attempt to explain how these partial screen-shots work together, but it is critical that you print out a copy of the entire *VIXCallHedge* spreadsheet tab for reference as you proceed through the VIX call hedging example in this chapter. I always reference the specific figure in the book, but it can be very cumbersome to repeatedly locate the appropriate exhibit. It will be much more efficient to refer to a separate printed sheet. This will also help you focus on the material. You might also find it instructive to simultaneously access the actual *VIXCallHedge* worksheet on your computer.

Explaining spreadsheet functionality in writing is challenging, as is absorbing operational instructions - especially when the concepts are new or unfamiliar. However, after a little hands-on experimentation, you should quickly become proficient with the spreadsheet and will find it very easy to use in practice. The primary functions are all automated and are accessed via push-button macros.

As a reminder, users may only enter or modify values in spreadsheet cells with a solid-blue background and white type. Most of the other cells are protected and may not be changed by the user. In addition, data validation rules apply to many cell values to preserve the integrity and validity of the calculations. In addition to modifying the values in cells with blue backgrounds, users may also use the macro buttons to execute macro functions.

## Hedge Objective

The first step in identifying the lowest cost hedging solution with VIX call options is to identify the hedge objective. In other words, how much profit would we need the hedge to generate if a catastrophic event occurred while holding our option strategy? In the iron condor example that we have used throughout this article, we planned to exit the strategy if total losses equaled 20% of the required capital. If we lost 100% of our iron condor required capital due to a catastrophic event, the hedge would need to generate a profit equal to 80% of our required capital. The 100% loss combined with the 80% gain would result in a net 20% loss of required capital, which would exactly equal our planned maximum loss.

Figure 4.3 is an image of the top-left section of the *VIXCallHedge* worksheet. All spreadsheet exhibits include row numbers and column letters to make it easier to find cell locations. This is particularly important in the *VIXCallHedge* worksheet, because the panes are split and frozen at cell F7, which means the columns range A:E and row range 1:6 are always visible.

The 80% hedge profit is entered in cell D4. In order to calculate the dollar gain, we also need to supply the total required capital for the iron condor, which you may recall was $106,712. This value is entered in cell D5. The resulting hedge objective would be to generate $85,370 ($106,712 X 80.0%) in the event of a catastrophic loss.

**Parameters**

| | | |
|---|---|---|
| Clear IVs | Calc IVs | 15   33 |
| RF Rt | 1.00% | |
| B/A Spd | 0.10 | |
| Analysis DT | 2/27/2017 | |
| RegT Hedge | 80.00% | |
| MaxIV | 200.0% | |
| User VIX Δ=> | 106,712 | |
| HP TDays> | 15 | |

| | 3/1/2017 | 3/8/2017 | 3/15/2017 | 3/22/2017 | 4/19/2017 |
|---|---|---|---|---|---|
| | 3 | 3 | 3 | 3 | 4 |
| Cal Days> | 2 | 9 | 16 | 23 | 51 |
| Trade Days> | 2 | 7 | 12 | 17 | 36 |

| TDTE VIX Δ | TDays | Yrs | Mid-F.Price | Instrument | VIX Change | Pct of VIX Δ | EndingVIX Δ | Hedge NC | Call Strike | Call Ask |
|---|---|---|---|---|---|---|---|---|---|---|
| 0 | 0 | 0.000 | 11.880 | VIX Index | 45.00 | 100.0% | 56.88 | NA | NA | NA |
| 1 | 2 | 0.008 | 11.925 | 3/1/2017 | 44.04 | 97.9% | 55.97 | 21.5 | 14.00 | 0.05 |
| 6 | 7 | 0.028 | 12.525 | 3/8/2017 | 34.09 | 75.7% | 46.61 | 27.0 | 18.00 | 0.05 |
| 9 | 12 | 0.048 | 12.950 | 3/15/2017 | 30.73 | 68.3% | 43.68 | 32.2 | 20.00 | 0.10 |
| 12 | 17 | 0.067 | 12.975 | 3/22/2017 | 40.88 | 90.8% | 53.86 | 37.9 | 22.00 | 0.15 |
| 21 | 36 | 0.143 | 14.975 | 4/19/2017 | 22.26 | 49.5% | 37.23 | 55.2 | 24.00 | 0.65 |
| 41 | 56 | 0.222 | 15.725 | 5/17/2017 | 15.61 | 34.7% | 31.34 | 100.7 | 25.00 | 1.00 |
| 65 | 80 | 0.317 | 16.325 | 6/21/2017 | 12.26 | 27.2% | 28.58 | 134.6 | 25.00 | 1.20 |
| 84 | 99 | 0.393 | 16.925 | 7/19/2017 | 10.92 | 24.3% | 27.85 | 151.6 | 25.00 | 1.35 |
| 104 | 119 | 0.472 | 17.225 | 8/16/2017 | 10.03 | 22.3% | 27.25 | 168.9 | 25.00 | 1.45 |
| 128 | 143 | 0.567 | | 9/20/2017 | 9.27 | 20.6% | | 0.0 | | 0.0 |
| 148 | 163 | 0.647 | | 10/18/2017 | 8.77 | 19.5% | | 0.0 | | 0.0 |
| 168 | 183 | 0.726 | | 11/15/2017 | 8.35 | 18.6% | | 0.0 | | 0.0 |

**Figure 4.3: VIX Call Hedge (LHS)**

Terms / Holidays / PositionSize / FuturesHedge / VIXCallHedge / EOPutHedge

# Catastrophic Risk Event

Now that we have entered our hedge objective into we need to define the impact of the black-swan ev Specifically, we need to estimate how much the V increase in response to the hypothetical event. Th important. It will help us select the strike prices of the VIX call options and it will also determine the expected profit from the hedge.

There is obviously no way to know the exact amount the VIX index would increase in advance, but we can gain some insight from history. In addition, after we calculate the hedge solution, we will use the *VIXCallHedge* worksheet as a scenario analysis tool, which will allow us to test the performance of our hedge solution in many different environments.

Let's revisit the VIX historical data in Figure 4.0. The early VIX index values were derived from S&P 100 (OEX) options. S&P 500 options were not used until 2003. The highest closing VIX value from 1990 to March 2017 was 80.86 (the 100th percentile), which occurred during the Great Recession of 2008.

The terrorist attacks on 9/11/2001 offer another black swan data point. The closing VIX index value on 9/10/2001 was 31.84. Unfortunately, the market was closed until 9/17/2001, and the closing VIX index value on that date was 41.76. The VIX index increased by less than 10 points, but this is very misleading. If the market had remained open, the VIX index would have spiked much higher. In addition, the initial VIX index value of 31.84 was already elevated (94th percentile) due to the economic recession of 1991.

The event that most closely captures the discrete price decline of a black-swan event was the 1987 crash. The VIX index was not created until 1993, but the CBOE was able to use historical OEX option data to calculate earlier VIX index values. The symbol for the VIX index derived from OEX options is VXO. VXO data is available from 1986 to the present.

VXO closed on Thursday 10/15/1986 at 27.86. It jumped to 36.37 on Friday before skyrocketing to 150.19 on Black Monday (10/19/1987): the highest VIX or VXO close ever recorded. On Tuesday, the VXO climbed even higher (intra-day) to 172.79 before closing at 140. The VXO traded above 100 for the next six trading days.

he S&P 500 index declined by over 20% on Black Monday, but ealized volatility remained very high throughout the following week. Several 10% daily SPX swings were recorded during that period. The persistent high level of *realized* volatility immediately following Black Monday explains why VXO remained at such extremes for an extended period.

With that historical background, let's return to the VIX estimate in the *VIXCallHedge* worksheet. In this example, I assumed the VIX would increase by 45 points, which is entered in cell F5 (Figure 4.3). We will review the procedure for entering market data in a subsequent section, but the VIX index would have increased from 11.88 (D7) to 56.88 (H7).

Given that VXO increased to over 150 during the 1987 crash, why assume that the VIX index would only increase by 45 points to 56.88? Because a 45-point increase is a more conservative estimate and we want to ensure that we are adequately protected. If the market was closed for a week (as it was after 9/11), we might miss the majority of the VIX spike and be unable to realize the full profit potential of our hedge.

There is no perfect forecast. The spreadsheet was designed to be an interactive tool. Ideally, many different scenarios should be considered before deciding on a specific hedge solution. As I promised earlier, we will use *VIXCallHedge* worksheet as a scenario analysis tool after we calculate the initial hedge solutions.

## Market Data

Before we can calculate the hedge solutions, we have a little more housekeeping work to do in the spreadsheet. We need to provide all of the market-related input data. Unless otherwise noted, all of the following spreadsheet cell locations refer to Figure 4.3.

The analysis date of 2/27/2017 is entered in cell F2 and represents the date the market prices were gathered *and* it also represents the initial entry date for the hedge transaction. This will always be the case; hedge solutions are only valid at current executable price levels. In this case, the analysis date also represents the entry date for the iron condor we discussed earlier.

The risk-free interest rate (1%) is used in the option pricing formulas and is entered in cell D2. The hedge solutions include slippage and commissions, both of which are user-input variables. The *actual* (not quoted) bid-ask spread (0.10) is entered in cell E2 and the commission cost per VIX option contract (0.70) is entered in cell S2 (*NOTE: Figure 4.4*).

We also need to enter the *number of trading days that will pass before the hypothetical black-swan event*, and the maximum total number of trading days we plan to maintain the hedge. At first glance, that seems ridiculous; we need to know the exact day the black-swan event is going to occur? Not exactly.

The spreadsheet will eventually calculate the effect of the black-swan event on each trading day during the holding period, but it loops through every trading day to do this calculation – one at a time. As a result, the spreadsheet requires an initial estimate of the number of days that will pass before the catastrophic event. I suggest using an initial value near the midpoint of the maximum holding period.

The maximum holding period for the hedge should correspond exactly with the maximum holding period for our iron condor position. In this case, I assumed we would exit the iron condor a minimum of five trading days before expiration. The April 2017 SPX options in the iron condor expire in 38 trading days, so the maximum holding period would be 33 trading days (38 − 5), which is entered in cell C5. I entered 15 (B5) for the number of days that would pass before the black-swan event.

We also need to enter the current VIX index value (D7) and mid-market pricing data for the VIX futures contracts (D8:D19), which are required to value VIX options. The *VIXCallHedge* worksheet automatically populated the cells E8:E19 with the expiration dates for the first four weekly VIX futures contracts and for the next eight VIX monthly futures contracts.

The same VIX futures settlement dates are shown in cells G2:R2 at the top of the worksheet. The corresponding number of calendar days and trading days (adjusted for data on the *Holidays* tab) for each contract are shown in cells G3:R3 and G4:R4 respectively.

You will note that the cell range D17:D19 is empty. Due to either liquidity or lack of availability, I did not include these values. This does not compromise the spreadsheet calculations. However, it is *always* necessary to include the current mid-market futures price for every corresponding option candidate with the same expiration date. In addition, while prices may be left empty at the bottom of the futures price list (D17:D19) if there are not corresponding VIX option candidates, *no missing prices or gaps are ever permitted in the middle of the futures price list, nor are missing prices ever permitted in the middle of the option price list. This would cause spreadsheet errors and/or compromise the results.*

The last market data input requirements are the VIX call option strike prices (J8:J19) and *actual* ask prices (K8:K19). The *actual* ask prices are not the *quoted* ask prices. They should represent where you can actually buy each respective VIX call option. The quoted ask prices may be higher.

You will note that the strike prices (J8:J19) are not the same for every option expiration date. Keep in mind that we need the VIX futures level (which is also the at-the-money level for each VIX option) to exceed the strike price of each option after the black-swan event. This guarantees that we will always be able to exit the VIX call hedge for a profit.

The spreadsheet uses the VIX futures volatility model presented earlier to estimate the VIX futures price changes (F7:F19) 15 trading days (B5) in the future that would correspond to each VIX call option candidate. When combined with the initial mid-market VIX index and futures values (D7:D19), the spreadsheet calculates the ending VIX index and VIX futures values (H7:H19) 15 trading days in the future. Each expected change in VIX futures price is also expressed as a percentage of the change in the VIX index (G7:G19). As you will recall, the relative VIX futures price changes are a declining non-linear function of the time-to-expiration.

However, if you look at the data in cells G7:G19, they do not decline uniformly. Instead, they even increase from 68.3% to 90.8% in cells G10 and G11. How is that possible? I will not go into great detail here, but the spreadsheet computations are more complex than they originally appear.

For example, imagine that we implemented the initial hedge with the VIX call option that expired on 3/22/2017 (row 11), 17 trading days in the future. If the black-swan event occurred in 15 trading days (B5), the VIX futures contract and VIX call option would only have two trading days left until expiration (A11). As a result, the volatility of the VIX futures contract with only two trading days remaining until expiration would increase sharply (G11).

Similarly, if we implemented the initial hedge with the VIX call option that expired on 3/8/2017 (row 9), it would initially have seven trading days remaining until expiration. However, it would expire worthless before the black-swan event, which would require us to purchase another (7-day) VIX call option, which would also expire worthless. Finally, we would purchase a third (7-day) VIX call option, which would have six trading days (A9) remaining until expiration when the black-swan event eventually occurred on the $15^{th}$ trading day. This would require a total of three separate VIX call option purchases (T9).

The spreadsheet does have a simplifying assumption. It assumes that a seven-day VIX call option would always be available to purchase at the expiration of the initial hedge position. While that is not a valid assumption, it does allow us to accurately calculate an unbiased estimate of the cost of implementing and maintaining the hedge using VIX call options with seven trading days remaining until expiration. In addition, the calculations use actual market prices, commissions, and slippage for every VIX call option candidate.

If you are interested in the intermediate spreadsheet calculations, go back and reread the above material, but understanding how the *VIXCallHedge* worksheet applies the VIX futures model in each hedge example is not required to use the spreadsheet in practice.

However, it is important to understand that we need the VIX futures level (which is also the at-the-money level for each VIX option) to exceed the strike price of each option after the black-swan event. As a result, it is important to review the VIX futures price forecasts (H7:H19) when selecting the strike prices for each VIX call option candidate. In the plus 45 point VIX index scenario, all of the VIX futures prices would exceed 27. As a result, I set a strike price ceiling of 25 for each of the VIX call option candidates.

You are probably asking why I used the lower strike prices for the options with the shortest time-to-expiration. For example, why did I select the VIX call option with the 14 strike for the option that expired on 3/1/2017? The reason is that VIX call options still trade in $0.05 increments (as do VIX futures), and all of the 3/1/2017 call options with strike prices of 14 and above were offered for $0.05. Obviously the call option with the lowest strike price was the best value. The same rationale was used when selecting the strikes for the other short-dated options.

I went into more detail in this section to satisfy the curiosity of more quantitative traders. However, knowledge of the specific calculation methodology is not required to use the spreadsheet. Here is a brief recap of the market data entry steps:

1. Enter the general market data: analysis date, risk-free interest rate, slippage, and commissions
2. Enter the two holding period values: trade days to black swan and maximum holding period
3. Enter the VIX index and VIX futures prices
4. Enter the VIX call option strikes and actual ask prices

I want to emphasize again that the *VIXCallHedge* worksheet is an interactive tool. Try different strike prices and experiment with the spreadsheet. Once you get comfortable with the spreadsheet, you will find it very easy to use.

## Option Valuation

We have entered all of the required input values and are ready to proceed to option valuation. As a result, we will now be concentrating on the right-side of the *VIXCallHedge* worksheet, which is depicted in Figure 4.4. Due to the split screen, you will note that columns A to E are still visible in Figure 4.4, but the next column shown is column L, which would actually be adjacent to the column K in Figure 4.3.

The only user-input required in this section is the maximum implied volatility (IV) value, which is entered in cell E4 (Figure 4.4). The next step in the process is to use the user-supplied market data to solve for the initial or current implied volatilities of the VIX call option candidates.

First, click on the "Clear IVs" push-button macro at the top-left of the *VIXCallHedge* worksheet. This will clear the initial implied volatility data (L8:L19), and it will also clear or zero-out the entire right-side of the spreadsheet (M8:S19), because all of these values are derived from the initial implied volatilities of the VIX call option candidates.

After clearing the initial implied volatilities, click on the "Calc IVs" push-button macro at the top-left of the *VIXCallHedge* worksheet. This will use the current market-data to calculate the initial implied volatilities for every candidate (L8:L19). To avoid erroneous IV values that usually result from invalid prices, the IV values will be capped at the maximum IV value (E4). If one or more initial IV values (L8:L19) equals the maximum IV value, verify that your pricing data is valid. If it is, consider increasing the maximum IV value (E4).

The *VIXCallHedge* worksheet will then automatically repopulate the columns on the right-side of the spreadsheet that are derived from the initial implied volatility values. The initial prices and implied volatilities represent the values at the inception of the hedge. Projected implied volatilities are calculated for two distinct future scenarios.

The first scenario assumes *no black-swan event occurs* during the entire holding period of the option strategy (C5). In the "no change" scenario, the VIX futures and VIX call options age by the lesser of 1) the actual number of trade days remaining until expiration for each option and 2) the maximum number of trading days specified in cell C5, 33 trade days in this case. In both cases, the initial volatility term structures remain unchanged. The projected "no change" implied volatilities are shown in the cell range M8:M19. The ending "no change" implied volatilities are used to calculate the ending "no change" call option values (O8:O19).

As you would expect, most of the out-of-the-money VIX call options expire worthless, except for a few of the longer-dated options that would still have some remaining time value at the end of 33 trading days. The changes in the option prices from the initial values to the ending "no change" values will be used to calculate the total cost of the hedge. Since black swan scenarios are rare, the ending "no change" scenario will predominate and we will repeatedly incur these hedging costs.

The second scenario assumes that *a black-swan event does occur* during the holding period, on the trading day specified in cell B5. In the "VIX change" scenario, the VIX futures and VIX call options age by the number of trading days specified in cell B5, 15 trading days in this case. In the black swan scenario, the initial VIX futures term structure changes considerably, but the ending implied VIX call option volatilities do not.

Clear IVs | Calc IVs

| | D | E | | | | | | | | | S |
|---|---|---|---|---|---|---|---|---|---|---|---|
| | RF Rt 1.00% | B/A Spd 0.10 | | | | | | | | | Com/C 0.70 |
| | RegT Hedge 80.00% | MaxIV 200.0% | | | | | | | | | |
| | 106,712 | User VIX Δ=> | | | | | | | | | |

HP TDays> — 15 | 33

Top strip (columns 5–11):

| | 5 | 6 | 7 | 8 | 9 | 10 | 11 |
|---|---|---|---|---|---|---|---|
| | 5/17/2017 | 6/21/2017 | 7/19/2017 | 8/16/2017 | 9/20/2017 | 10/18/2017 | 11/15/2017 |
| | 79 | 114 | 142 | 170 | 205 | 233 | 261 |
| | 56 | 80 | 99 | 119 | 143 | 163 | 183 |
| | 15.61 | 12.26 | 10.92 | 10.03 | 9.27 | 8.77 | 8.35 |

Main table:

| TDTE VIX Δ | TDays | Yrs | Mid-F.Price | Instrument | Initial IV | EndIV NoChg | EndIV VIXΔ | Call NoChg | VIX Call Δ | Call Δ Profit | Avg. Profit | TCost/TD | # Hdg.Trds | Avg % Δ |
|---|---|---|---|---|---|---|---|---|---|---|---|---|---|---|
| 0 | 0 | 0.000 | 11.880 | VIX Index | NA | NA | NA | NA | NA | NA | NA | NA | NA | 100.0% |
| 1 | 2 | 0.008 | 11.925 | 3/1/2017 | 126.1% | 126.1% | 126.1% | 0.00 | 41.87 | 89,023 | 85,503 | 61.3 | 8 | 94.4% |
| 6 | 7 | 0.028 | 12.525 | 3/8/2017 | 124.2% | 126.1% | 124.6% | 0.00 | 28.52 | 76,514 | 85,394 | 22.0 | 3 | 83.5% |
| 9 | 12 | 0.048 | 12.950 | 3/15/2017 | 124.1% | 126.1% | 124.2% | 0.00 | 23.59 | 75,248 | 85,360 | 28.7 | 2 | 76.3% |
| 2 | 17 | 0.067 | 12.975 | 3/22/2017 | 131.3% | 126.1% | 126.1% | 0.00 | 31.76 | 119,745 | 85,369 | 35.0 | 1 | 70.8% |
| 21 | 36 | 0.143 | 14.975 | 4/19/2017 | 119.6% | 125.7% | 128.8% | 0.00 | 13.79 | 72,451 | 85,320 | 109.9 | 1 | 53.6% |
| 41 | 56 | 0.222 | 15.725 | 5/17/2017 | 108.8% | 127.6% | 116.9% | 0.32 | 8.92 | 79,630 | 85,367 | 210.8 | 1 | 36.1% |
| 65 | 80 | 0.317 | 16.325 | 6/21/2017 | 92.1% | 113.7% | 102.5% | 0.94 | 7.40 | 83,308 | 85,350 | 110.8 | 1 | 27.7% |
| 84 | 99 | 0.393 | 16.925 | 7/19/2017 | 81.9% | 101.8% | 89.9% | 1.24 | 6.89 | 83,778 | 85,342 | 57.0 | 1 | 24.5% |
| 104 | 119 | 0.472 | 17.225 | 8/16/2017 | 74.7% | 88.9% | 80.1% | 1.34 | 6.45 | 84,202 | 85,358 | 63.5 | 1 | 22.4% |
| 128 | 143 | 0.567 | | 9/20/2017 | | | | | | 0 | 0 | | 1 | 20.7% |
| 148 | 163 | 0.647 | | 10/18/2017 | | | | | | 0 | 0 | | 1 | 19.6% |
| 168 | 183 | 0.726 | | 11/15/2017 | | | | | | 0 | 0 | | 1 | 18.6% |

**Figure 4.4: VIX Call Hedge (LHS)**

Terms  Holidays  PositionSize  FuturesHedge  VIXCallHedge  EOPutHedge

VIX implied volatilities are remarkably stable, even in wildly different volatility environments. The VIX call options still age, but the initial term structure of implied volatilities remains relatively stable. The projected "VIX change" implied volatilities are shown in the cell range N8:N19. The ending "VIX change" implied volatilities are used to calculate the ending black swan call option values (P8:P19) after the specified number of trading days in the future (B5).

As intended, all of the VIX call options increase significantly in value. The changes in the option prices from the initial values to the ending "VIX change" values will be used to calculate the hedge profits.

As discussed earlier, the spreadsheet will eventually calculate the effect of the black-swan event on *each* trading day during the holding period. It will loop through every trading day in the holding period to do this calculation – one trading day at a time. As a result, the spreadsheet only depicts the implied volatilities, option values, and hedge profits for a single black-swan event date.

The *VIXCallHedge* worksheet will use the hedge profits in conjunction with the hedge objective to determine the required number of VIX call option contracts to purchase for each candidate. The number of required contracts (the hedge solution) is required to calculate the average profits and the total costs per day of each hedge. We will review the procedure required to generate the hedge solutions in the next section.

## Hedge Solution

This section will reference the left-side (Figure 5.1), right-side (Figure 5.2), and bottom-left section (Figure 5.3) of the *EQPutHedge* worksheet. This section will reference the left-side (Figure 4.3), right-side (Figure 4.4), and the bottom-left portion (Figure 4.5) of the *VIXCallHedge* worksheet. Due to the split-screen, rows one through six are also shown in Figure 4.5.

After calculating the ending implied volatilities and option values for the "no change" and "VIX change" scenarios in the previous section, we only need one additional set of values to complete the remaining *VIXCallHedge* spreadsheet calculations: the number of VIX call option contracts required (I8:I19 in Figure 4.3).

There is only one additional user input value required in this section. The *VIXCallHedge* spreadsheet can calculate the hedge solutions based on the black swan scenario profits on a *single event date* (B5) or on the *average black swan scenario profits* over every date in the holding period (C5). The *profit type* user-variable is entered in a drop-down box in cell E23 (Figure 4.5). The *"Scenario"* option uses the profit from the single scenario date (B5) and the *"Average"* option uses the average black swan profits over every date in the holding period (C5). While looking at hedge solutions based on specific scenario dates can be interesting, users will predominately solve for hedge solutions using the *average* black swan profit over all holding period dates.

This creates a little bit of a chicken and egg problem. We cannot calculate the average profits without knowing the number of contracts to purchase, but that is exactly what we are trying to determine in this section. The hedge solutions shown in Figure 4.4 represent the required number of contracts (rounded to the first decimal place) to satisfy the hedge objective based on the *average* black swan profits during the holding period.

However, the hedge solutions (I8:I19 in Figure 4.3) are only calculated when the appropriate macro is executed. These values are not continuously re-calculated in the spreadsheet. As a result, when you open the spreadsheet, the hedge solution values (I8:I19 in Figure 4.3) will not be applicable to your current hedging problem. In addition, some may be missing or zero. Regardless, the spreadsheet needs a set of sample hedge values in order to calculate and re-calibrate the average profit values.

You could enter a set of sample hedge values by hand, but I created a macro that automatically populates the cells I8:I19 (Figure 4.3) with sample solution values of ten contracts. To populate these cells, click on the push-button macro "Populate Sample Hedge Values." This macro will also zero-out the average profit values (R8:R19 in Figure 4.4), because the spreadsheet recognizes that the average profit values are dependent on the hedge solution values (I8:I19 in Figure 4.3). The macro will also clear the related profit values in cells W8:Z19 (not shown). Since we changed the number of contracts, the old average profit values are no longer valid.

Before calculating the actual number of contracts required, we must recalculate the average black swan profit values (R8:R19 in Figure 4.4) for the sample number of contracts (I8:I19 in Figure 4.4).

Click on the "Calc Average VIX Change Profit" push-button macro (Figure 4.5) to calculate the average black swan profit. The macro will calculate the black swan scenario profit for every trading day in the holding period and then calculate the average of these values. The new average profit values will be saved in cells R8:R19 (Figure 4.4).

We are finally ready to calculate the *actual* hedge solutions based on the *average* black swan profits for the entire holding period. Select *"Average"* from the drop-down list in cell E23 (Figure 4.5) and then click on the "Calc Hedge NC" push-button macro (Figure 4.5). This will calculate the number of contracts (I8:I19) required to satisfy the hedge objective (D4:D5) based on the average black swan profits (R8:R19 in Figure 4.4) over the entire holding period (C5).

As you might have guessed, since we changed the number of contracts, the macro cleared the average profit values again. Rerun the "Calc Average VIX Change Profit" macro (Figure 4.5) to calculate the revised average black swan profit values. Now all of the spreadsheet cells will be populated for each of the call option candidates. Note that the re-calculated average black swan profit values (R8:R19 in Figure 4.4) range from $85,320 to $85,503, which are all almost exactly equal to the hedge profit objective of $85,370 (106,712 X 80%). The average profit variation is due to rounding the number of contracts to the first decimal place.

Before examining the individual hedge solutions, I want to point out that you can also manually round the number of contracts to the nearest whole number before re-calculating the average black swan profit values. I intentionally *did not* round these values in this article, because I wanted to make the final solutions as intuitive as possible. In addition, I wanted to illustrate that the hedge solutions would all satisfy the specified hedge profit objective. In practice, rounded values are required to accurately calculate hedge costs and profits.

The detailed explanation with specific cell references can make the process seem overly complicated. It is actually quite simple.

To calculate the hedge solution based on the average black swan profit:
1. Click on the "Populate Sample Hedge Values" button,
2. Click on the "Calc Average VIX Change Profit" button,
3. Select "Average" from the drop down-list (E23 in Figure 4.5),
4. Click on the "Calc Hedge NC" button, and
5. Click on the "Calc Average VIX Change Profit" button. ·

| | A | B | C | D | E |
|---|---|---|---|---|---|
| 1 | | | | RF Rt | B/A Spd |
| 2 | Clear | | Calc | 1.00% | 0.10 |
| 3 | IVs | | IVs | RegT Hedge | MaxIV |
| 4 | | | | 80.00% | 200.0% |
| 5 | HP TDays> | 15 | 33 | 106,712 | User VIX Δ=> |
| 6 | TDTE VIX Δ | TDays | Yrs | Mid-F.Price | Instrument |
| 21 | **Figure 4.5: VIX Call Hedge (Macros)** | | | | |
| 22 | **Calc Hedge NC** | | | | Profit Type: |
| 23 | | | | | Average |
| 24 | **Calc Average VIX Change Profit** | | | | |
| 25 | | | | | |
| 26 | **Populate Sample Hedge Values** | | | | |
| 27 | | | | | |

VIXCallHedge / EQPutHedge

The goal of this chapter is to identify the most efficient *VIX call option hedge* to mitigate the risk of random catastrophic events. The VIX call option with the lowest total cost per trade day (S8:S19 in Figure 4.4) is the most efficient hedging solution. The VIX call option hedge solution with the lowest cost per trade day (including slippage and commissions) requires the purchase of 27 VIX call options with an expiration date of 3/8/2017 and a strike price of 18 (Figure 4.3). The total hedging cost per day (including slippage and commissions) is $22.0 (Cell S9 in Figure 4.4).

Since this call option expires in seven trading days, the hedge solution also assumes that this same option (with seven trading days remaining until expiration) would be repurchased repeatedly during the option strategy holding period to maintain the desired level of catastrophic risk protection.

The cumulative cost of maintaining the lowest cost hedge solution over the entire 33 trading-day holding period would be $726 ($22 per trading day X 33 trading days). This would reduce the profitability of each iron condor trade by 0.68% ($726 / $106,712).

The good news is that even for a conventional option income strategy (OIS) without the benefits of any entry timing filters, the

15,434 OIS trades (reported in *Option Income Strategy Trade Filters*) earned an average return of 3.22% on required capital (after commissions). Filtered option income strategies could potentially double the average return per trade, which would easily generate sufficient income to absorb the incremental cost of the catastrophic risk hedge. The cumulative hedging cost should always be included when entering, evaluating, and developing option strategies.

Perhaps the most alarming observation in Figure 4.4 is the wide variation in hedging costs across the VIX call option candidates. The total hedge cost per trading day ranged from a low of $22.0 to a high of $210.8 (S8:S19). The large variation in costs is influenced by the unique characteristics of the term structure of volatilities, which are not well understood – especially when applied to VIX option hedging solutions.

Daily costs at the high end of the range would increase cumulative hedging costs to $6,956.40 ($210.8 X 33). This would reduce the profitability of each iron condor trade by 6.52% ($6,956.40 / $106,712). The cost of choosing the wrong hedging candidate could easily compromise the profitability of even the best option strategies. This does not necessarily imply that VIX call options are mispriced; it only demonstrates that the hedging candidates are definitely not equally-suited for satisfying our specific hedging objectives.

## Scenario Analysis

In the previous section, we solved for the number of contracts required to meet our hedge profit objective based on the average profit. To calculate average profit, the macro begins with a value of zero in cell B5, which generates the hedge profit from the 45-point increase in the VIX index, which occurs immediately (on trade day 0). The macro then repeats the hedge profit calculation for trading days one through 33, then calculates the average profit for the entire holding period. The average profits for the VIX call candidates are provided in cells R8:R19 (Figure 4.4) of the *VIXCallHedge* worksheet.

As explained earlier, the hedge profits can vary significantly depending on when the black-swan event actually occurs. When I began using this spreadsheet for hedging purposes, I found that I wanted more information about the hedge profits from events occurring over the entire range of trading days. I initially changed the trading day the event occurred (B5) manually and observed the revised hedge profits, but this was tedious and not very practical.

As a result, I modified the "Calc Average VIX Change Profit" macro. The revised macro now calculates the average profit, minimum profit, maximum profit, and profit range for black-swan events occurring over each trading day in the holding period. These values are provided in cells W8:Z19 of the *VIXCallHedge* worksheet (not shown).

I compiled these results in Figure 4.6, along with the total hedge cost per day that we calculated in the previous section. As you will recall, the VIX call option hedge solution with the lowest cost per trade day (including slippage and commissions) requires the purchase of 27 VIX call options with an expiration date of 3/8/2017 and a strike price of 18.

The average, minimum, and maximum hedge profits for the lowest cost hedge are $85,394, $72,931, and $103,693, respectively. The resulting max-min range was $30,762. As you can see, the range is significant, but it is not unusual – at least with respect to the ranges of the other candidates.

The next lowest cost solution was the VIX call option with an expiration date of 3/15/2017 and a strike price of 20. The total cost per day was approximately 30% higher than the lowest cost solution ($28.7 versus $22.0) and the profit range was almost 70% higher ($52,168 versus $30,762). I suggest reviewing the average profit, minimum profit, maximum profit, and the profit range when deciding on your desired hedge candidate.

Now that we have solved for the hedge solutions for each VIX call option candidate, we can also use the *VIXCallHedge* worksheet as a scenario analysis tool. We originally assumed that the VIX index would increase by 45 points in response to a discrete catastrophic event. The hedge solutions were derived from this VIX index forecast. We can now examine how our hedge would perform if the VIX index were to change by a different amount.

## Figure 4.6: VIX Call Hedge, Scenario Profits for Events on Trade Days 0 - 33

| Instrument | Hedge NC | Call Strike | TCost/TD | Avg. Profit | Min Profit | Max Profit | Profit Range |
|---|---|---|---|---|---|---|---|
| VIX Index | NA | NA | NA | NA | NA | NA | NA |
| 3/1/2017 | 21.5 | 14.00 | 61.3 | 85,503 | 81,125 | 89,880 | 8,756 |
| 3/8/2017 | 27.0 | 18.00 | 22.0 | 85,394 | 72,931 | 103,693 | 30,762 |
| 3/15/2017 | 32.2 | 20.00 | 28.7 | 85,360 | 66,264 | 118,432 | 52,168 |
| 3/22/2017 | 37.9 | 22.00 | 35.0 | 85,369 | 58,007 | 131,722 | 73,715 |
| 4/19/2017 | 55.2 | 24.00 | 109.9 | 85,320 | 49,826 | 159,597 | 109,771 |
| 5/17/2017 | 100.7 | 25.00 | 210.8 | 85,367 | 65,941 | 119,373 | 53,432 |
| 6/21/2017 | 134.6 | 25.00 | 110.8 | 85,350 | 72,941 | 100,937 | 27,996 |
| 7/19/2017 | 151.6 | 25.00 | 57.0 | 85,342 | 75,792 | 97,089 | 21,297 |
| 8/16/2017 | 168.9 | 25.00 | 63.5 | 85,358 | 78,553 | 93,876 | 15,323 |
| 9/20/2017 | 0.0 | NA | NA | NA | NA | NA | NA |
| 10/18/2017 | 0.0 | NA | NA | NA | NA | NA | NA |
| 11/15/2017 | 0.0 | NA | NA | NA | NA | NA | NA |

The left-side of Figure 4.7 describes each VIX call option candidate solution: expiration date, number of contracts, strike price, and total hedge cost per trading day. The right side of Figure 4.7 shows the average profit for several VIX index scenarios: VIX+20, VIX+30, VIX+45, VIX+60, VIX+70, and the average over all scenarios. To calculate the average hedge profits for each scenario, enter the desired change in the VIX index in cell F5 of the *VIXCallHedge* worksheet and then click on the "Calc Average VIX Change Profit" push-button macro (Figure 4.5). The macro will calculate the new average profit, minimum profit, maximum profit, and profit range for the new VIX index scenario.

Note that we did not change the hedge solution. We are using the scenario analysis tool to evaluate how our proposed hedge solution would perform in different volatility environments. As we would expect, the hedge solutions generated much lower average profits in the VIX+20 and VIX+30 scenarios. However, in these scenarios, the iron condor losses might not have been as extreme. This tool should be used in conjunction with your options analytical platform to evaluate the combined position.

For the VIX+60 and VIX+70 scenarios, the average hedge profits would have increased significantly - enough to guarantee a profit for the aggregate position, even after losing 100% of the required capital on the iron condor.

Take a look at the VIX call option expiring on 3/22/2017. The total cost of the hedge per day would have been approximately 23% higher than our lowest cost solution (35.0 versus 22.0), but the average scenario profit would have also been substantially higher ($105,959 versus $80,269). Does that mean that we should consider the 3/22/2017 option as well?

No, the hedge is designed to protect us in the case of a discrete catastrophic event, not to generate excess profits. Keep in mind that the daily probability of such an event is extremely small. Earlier we assumed a daily probability of only one out of 1000. As a result, we should not assign too much weight to the extreme VIX scenarios that exceed our best VIX index estimate.

## Figure 4.7: VIX Call Hedge, Average Profits for VIX Change Scenarios

| Instrument | Hedge NC | Call Strike | TCost/TD | VIX+20 | VIX+30 | VIX+45 | VIX+60 | VIX+70 | Avg, ALL |
|---|---|---|---|---|---|---|---|---|---|
| VIX Index | NA | NA | NA | NA | NA | NA | NA | NA | NA |
| 3/1/2017 | 21.5 | 14.00 | 61.3 | 34,783 | 55,071 | 85,503 | 120,587 | 141,630 | 87,515 |
| 3/8/2017 | 27.0 | 18.00 | 22.0 | 29,359 | 51,758 | 85,394 | 107,192 | 127,644 | 80,269 |
| 3/15/2017 | 32.2 | 20.00 | 28.7 | 25,411 | 49,094 | 85,360 | 108,231 | 130,222 | 79,664 |
| 3/22/2017 | 37.9 | 22.00 | 35.0 | 21,302 | 45,907 | 85,369 | 171,393 | 205,825 | 105,959 |
| 4/19/2017 | 55.2 | 24.00 | 109.9 | 21,053 | 44,739 | 85,320 | 111,179 | 137,851 | 80,029 |
| 5/17/2017 | 100.7 | 25.00 | 210.8 | 23,667 | 45,413 | 85,367 | 122,133 | 152,631 | 85,842 |
| 6/21/2017 | 134.6 | 25.00 | 110.8 | 27,896 | 48,545 | 85,350 | 124,161 | 153,644 | 87,919 |
| 7/19/2017 | 151.6 | 25.00 | 57.0 | 29,383 | 49,689 | 85,342 | 123,713 | 152,525 | 88,130 |
| 8/16/2017 | 168.9 | 25.00 | 63.5 | 29,535 | 49,876 | 85,358 | 124,139 | 152,968 | 88,375 |
| 9/20/2017 | 0.0 | NA | NA | NA | NA | NA | NA | NA | NA |
| 10/18/2017 | 0.0 | NA | NA | NA | NA | NA | NA | NA | NA |
| 11/15/2017 | 0.0 | NA | NA | NA | NA | NA | NA | NA | NA |

Instead, we should focus on the VIX+20 and VIX+30 scenarios, where the VIX call hedge is less effective. The 3/8/2017 call option dominates the 3/22/2017 candidate in both of these scenarios. In other words, it offers more protection or higher hedge profits at a lower cost. Finally, the 3/8/2017 option also had a much narrower profit range over all trading days than the 3/22/2017 option ($30,672 versus $73,715 in Figure 4.6). The 3/8/2017 call option dominates all other VIX call option candidates.

## Summary

We covered a lot of material in this chapter. The *VIXCallHedge* worksheet is a very powerful interactive tool. However, the spreadsheet does most of the work and all of the functions are automated.

In summary, there are six principal components of the *VIXCallHedge* spreadsheet:

1. Hedge Objective,
2. Catastrophic Risk Event,
3. Market Data,
4. Option Valuation,
5. Hedge Solution, and
6. Scenario Analysis

The best way to become proficient with the spreadsheet is to experiment. Concentrate on each component in order. I suggest using the original data set for practice. This will reduce the possibility of generating any data-related errors. As you become more proficient, begin experimenting with actual market data

# 5 - HEDGING: UNDERLYING PUT OPTIONS

Using volatility derivatives (VIX call options) to hedge random catastrophic events is a logical tactic, but there is a more direct hedging approach. Buying deep out-of-the-money put options on the underlying security (SPX) should always be explored as a potentially lower-cost alternative. The hedging costs and scenario results for both approaches should be compared to identify the most efficient hedging strategy in the specific market environment.

The *EQPutHedge* spreadsheet outlined in this chapter uses the same analytical framework as the *VIXCallHedge* spreadsheet from Chapter 4. In addition, the formats of the two spreadsheet tabs are almost identical. This was by design. The common analytical frameworks and spreadsheet layouts should make it easier for the user to become proficient with both worksheet tabs.

In addition, the SPX put hedge example in this chapter should provide a review of the *VIXCallHedge* spreadsheet's operational procedures. Since this chapter is partially a review, it will not provide the same level of detail as Chapter 4. Finally, the real-time market data in the VIX call and SPX put examples were retrieved simultaneously. As a result, the hedging results for both examples are realistic and are directly comparable.

## SPX Put Hedge Spreadsheet Overview

This section will provide a brief overview of the *EQPutHedge* spreadsheet, which should make it easier to understand the steps required to use the spreadsheet in practice, which we will cover in detail in the following sections. The objective of the *EQPutHedge* spreadsheet is to calculate the total dollar cost of the hedge per trade-day for a list of weekly and monthly SPX put options. These values can then be compared for all option candidates to identify the most cost-efficient hedging solution.

The *EQPutHedge* spreadsheet has the same six principal components as the *VIXCallHedge* spreadsheet from Chapter 4:

1. Hedge Objective,
2. Catastrophic Risk Event,
3. Market Data,
4. Option Valuation,
5. Hedge Solution, and
6. Scenario Analysis

We will review each of these components in detail in the following sections. The *EQPutHedge* spreadsheet has the same display size limitations as the *VIXCallHedge* spreadsheet. As a result, we will again use partial images of the *EQPutHedge* spreadsheet tab in this chapter.

As I strongly suggested earlier, it is critical that you print out a copy of the entire *EQPutHedge* spreadsheet tab for reference as you proceed through the hedging SPX put example in this chapter. I always reference the specific figure in the book, but it can be very cumbersome to repeatedly locate the appropriate exhibit. It will be much more efficient to refer to a separate printed sheet. This will also help you focus on the material. You might also find it instructive to simultaneously access the actual *EQPutHedge* worksheet on your computer.

## Hedge Objective

The process for entering the hedge objective in the *EQPutHedge* worksheet is identical to the process used in the *VIXCallHedge* spreadsheet from Chapter 4. The corresponding input values are also identical. Figure 5.1 is an image of the top-left section of the *EQPutHedge* worksheet.

The desired 80% hedge profit is entered in cell D4. In order to calculate the dollar gain, we also need to supply the total required capital for the iron condor ($106,712). This value is entered in cell D5. The resulting hedge objective would be to generate $85,370 ($106,712 X 80.0%) in the event of a catastrophic loss.

**Parameter block**

| | | C | D | E | F |
|---|---|---|---|---|---|
| Clear IVs | Calc IVs | IV/PRC | RF Rt | B/A Spd | Analysis DT |
| | | -1.2400 | 1.00% | 0.10 | 2/27/2017 |
| | | 27.7% | RegT Hedge | MaxIV | Cal Days> |
| | | 87.2% | 80.00% | 50.0% | Trade Days> |
| HP TDays> | 15 | 33 | 106,712 | EQ Index Δ | -20.00% |

**Expiration columns (G–K)**

| | G | H | I | J | K |
|---|---|---|---|---|---|
| | 3 | 3 | 3 | 3 | 4 |
| | 3/3/2017 | 3/10/2017 | 3/17/2017 | 3/24/2017 | 4/21/2017 |
| Cal Days> | 4 | 11 | 18 | 25 | 53 |
| Trade Days> | 4 | 9 | 14 | 19 | 38 |
| EQ Index Δ | -473.06 | -472.88 | -472.69 | -472.51 | -471.80 |

**Main data table**

| TDTE VIX Δ | TDays | Yrs | EQ Index | Instrument | Change | Pct of IV Δ | Ending Val | Hedge NP | Put Strike | Put Ask |
|---|---|---|---|---|---|---|---|---|---|---|
| 0 | 0 | 0.000 | 2,366.040 | EQ Index | -473.208 | 100.0% | 1,892.832 | NA | NA | NA |
| 1 | 4 | 0.016 | 2,365.300 | 3/3/2017 | -473.060 | 97.9% | 1,892.240 | 3.5 | 2,135.00 | 0.10 |
| 3 | 9 | 0.036 | 2,364.376 | 3/10/2017 | -472.875 | 86.0% | 1,891.501 | 4.0 | 2,100.00 | 0.30 |
| 13 | 14 | 0.056 | 2,363.452 | 3/17/2017 | -472.690 | 60.5% | 1,890.762 | 6.4 | 2,000.00 | 0.40 |
| 4 | 19 | 0.075 | 2,362.528 | 3/24/2017 | -472.506 | 82.1% | 1,890.023 | 6.2 | 2,000.00 | 0.70 |
| 23 | 38 | 0.151 | 2,359.022 | 4/21/2017 | -471.804 | 47.3% | 1,887.217 | 5.9 | 2,000.00 | 2.20 |
| 43 | 58 | 0.230 | 2,355.336 | 5/19/2017 | -471.067 | 33.8% | 1,884.269 | 5.4 | 2,000.00 | 5.00 |
| 62 | 77 | 0.306 | 2,351.841 | 6/16/2017 | -470.368 | 27.9% | 1,881.472 | 5.1 | 2,000.00 | 9.15 |
| 86 | 101 | 0.401 | 2,347.432 | 7/21/2017 | -469.486 | 24.0% | 1,877.946 | 4.9 | 2,000.00 | 15.90 |
| 106 | 121 | 0.480 | 2,343.765 | 8/18/2017 | -468.753 | 22.1% | 1,875.012 | 0.0 | | |
| 125 | 140 | 0.556 | 2,340.286 | 9/15/2017 | -468.057 | 20.8% | 1,872.229 | 0.0 | | |
| 150 | 165 | 0.655 | 2,335.717 | 10/20/2017 | -467.143 | 19.4% | 1,868.574 | 0.0 | | |
| 170 | 185 | 0.734 | 2,332.068 | 11/17/2017 | -466.414 | 18.5% | 1,865.654 | 0.0 | | |

Figure 5.1: SPX Put Hedge (LHS)

Terms / Holidays / PostionSize / FuturesHedge / VIXCallHedge / EQPutHedge

# Catastrophic Risk Event

Now that we have entered our hedge objective into the worksheet, we need to define the impact of the black-swan event on the S&P 500 index (SPX). Specifically, we need to estimate how much SPX would *decrease* in response to the hypothetical event. Unlike the last chapter, we need to estimate the percentage *decline* in SPX, instead of the point *increase* in the VIX index. The estimated SPX value *after the event* will help us select the strike prices of SPX put options. It will also determine the expected profit from the hedge.

There is obviously no way to know the exact amount SPX would decrease in advance, but we can gain some insight from history, as we did in the last chapter. After we calculate the hedge solution, we will use the *EQPutHedge* worksheet as a scenario analysis tool, which will allow us to evaluate the performance of our hedge solution in several different extreme environments.

In response to the terrorist attacks on 9/11/2001, SPX declined by only 4.9% from 9/10/2001 to 9/17/2001 (when the market reopened). If the market had remained open immediately after 9/11, SPX would have plummeted. In addition, SPX values were already depressed due to the economic recession of 2001, which probably dampened the initial response to the terrorist event. SPX declined by a total of 11.6% from 9/10/2001 to 9/21/2001, which reflects the cumulative market impact of the event.

The event that most closely captures the discrete price decline of a black-swan event was the 1987 stock market crash. SPX declined by 20.4% on Black Monday and declined by a cumulative 31.4% over five trading days.

With that historical background, let's return to the SPX estimate in the *EQPutHedge* worksheet. In this example, I assumed SPX would decrease by 20%, which is entered in cell F5 (Figure 5.1). Despite the fact that SPX declined by 31% over a five-day period in the 1987 crash, I chose to use the more conservative down 20% estimate, which was also more consistent with the one-day decline on Black Monday. We will review the procedure for entering market data in the following section, but SPX would have decreased from $2,366.04 (D7) to $1,892.832 (H7) in this example.

## Market Data

Before we can calculate the hedge solutions, we need to provide all of the market-related input data. Unless otherwise noted, all of the following spreadsheet cell locations refer to Figure 5.1. There are market data similarities to the *VIXCallHedge* spreadsheet, but there are also some important differences.

The same analysis date of 2/27/2017 is entered in cell F2 and represents the date the market prices were gathered *and* it also represents the initial entry date for the hedge transaction. In this case, the analysis date also represents the entry date for the iron condor we discussed earlier.

The same risk-free interest rate (1%) is used in the option pricing formulas and is entered in cell D2. The hedge solutions include slippage and commissions, both of which are user-input variables. The *actual* (not quoted) bid-ask spread (0.10) is entered in cell E2 and the commission cost per SPX option contract (1.00) is entered in cell S2 (*NOTE: Figure 5.2*).

There are also two new market data input values that are specific to the *EQPutHedge* worksheet. The SPX annualized dividend yield (1.97%) is entered in cell S4 (*NOTE: Figure 5.2*), which is used to adjust the forward price of SPX (D8:D19) for use in the option valuation formulas.

The slope of the implied volatility / SPX price function (-1.2400) is entered in cell C2 (Figure 5.1). This value might seem familiar. The negative 1.24 value was reduced by a scale-factor of 100 for use in the *EQPutHedge* spreadsheet, but it is the same slope (β or Beta) term that we solved for in the linear regression model in Chapter 4. The linear regression used daily closing prices from 2004 to February 2017.

$$VIX_T - VIX_{T-1} = \beta * LN\ (SPX_T/SPX_{T-1}) + \varepsilon$$

You will recall that we used the regression equation in Chapter 4 to solve for the change in the VIX index, for a given change in SPX. We will now use the same regression equation to solve for the change in the implied volatility of SPX options.

$$IV_T - IV_{T-1} = \beta * LN\ (SPX_T/SPX_{T-1}) + \varepsilon$$
$$IV_T - IV_{T-1} = -1.24 * LN\ (SPX_T/SPX_{T-1}) + \varepsilon$$

$IV_T$: **Implied Volatility Time T**
$IV_{T-1}$: **Implied Volatility Time T-1 (one day earlier)**
$\beta$: **Beta or slope coefficient**
**LN: Natural Log Function**
$\varepsilon$: **error term**

$SPX_T$: **SPX Price Time T**
$SPX_{T-1}$: **SPX Price Time T-1 (one day earlier)**

Knowing the percentage change in SPX due to the black-swan event is not sufficient to value the put options used in the hedge. We also need to estimate the change in the implied volatilities of those put options if the black-swan event occurred, which is why we need to use the regression equation. I will discuss this again later in this chapter, but the estimated 20% decline would generate a 27.7% increase in the implied volatility of near-term SPX put options. This value is calculated automatically in cell C3 and is derived from the user-input values in C2 (-1.24) and F5 (-20%).

Note, both of these values (C2: -1.24 and F5: -20%) may be modified by the user. However, please remember that the negative 1.24 slope coefficient in cell C2 was derived from the actual 2004 to 2017 data.

$$IV_T - IV_{T-1} = \beta * LN\ (SPX_T/SPX_{T-1}) + \varepsilon$$
$$IV_T - IV_{T-1} = -1.24 * LN\ (80\%)$$
$$IV_T - IV_{T-1} = -1.24 * LN\ (0.80)$$
$$IV_T - IV_{T-1} = -1.24 * -0.22314$$
$$IV_T - IV_{T-1} = 0.2767$$
$$IV_T - IV_{T-1} = 27.67\% \text{ (rounded to 27.7\% in Cell C3)}$$

We also need to enter the *number of trading days that will pass before the hypothetical black-swan event* (15 in cell B5), and the maximum total number of trading days we plan to maintain the hedge (33 in cell C5). These are exactly the same concepts (and values) used in the *VIXCallHedge* spreadsheet and they have the same exact meanings. As a result, I will not explain these terms again in this chapter.

We also need to enter the current SPX price (D7), but we *do not* need to enter the forward SPX values in cells D8:D19. These values are automatically derived from the dividend yield value in cell S4 (note: Figure 5.2). This represents a material difference between the *EQPutHedge* and *VIXCallHedge* worksheet. You will recall that we had to supply the mid-market pricing data for the VIX futures contracts in the *VIXCallHedge* spreadsheet, which were required to value VIX options. Instead, the SPX forward prices (D8:D19) are required to value SPX put options and they are calculated automatically by the spreadsheet.

The *EQPutHedge* worksheet automatically populated the cells E8:E19 with the expiration dates for the first four SPX weekly option contracts and for the next eight SPX monthly option contracts. The same SPX option expiration dates are shown in cells G2:R2 at the top of the worksheet. The corresponding number of calendar days and trading days (adjusted for data on the *Holidays* tab) for each contract are shown in cells G3:R3 and G4:R4 respectively.

The last market data input requirements are the SPX put option strike prices (J8:J19) and *actual* ask prices (K8:K19). The *actual* ask prices are not the *quoted* ask prices. They should represent where you can actually buy each respective SPX put option. The quoted ask prices may be higher. *No missing prices or gaps are ever permitted in the middle of the option price list. This would cause spreadsheet errors and/or compromise the results.*

You will note that the strike prices (J8:J19) are not the same for every option expiration date, but they are very similar. The differences are due to the discrete ask prices for each option. Ideally, the expected SPX price after the hypothetical black-swan event should be *lower* than the strike prices we chose for our SPX put option candidates. This ensures that each SPX put option will be in the money after such an event, which guarantees that we will always be able to exit the SPX put hedge for a profit, regardless when the event occurs during the holding period.

Here is a brief recap of the market data entry steps:
1. Enter the general market data: analysis date, risk-free interest rate, slippage, commissions, dividend yield, and IV/price beta
2. Enter the two holding period values: trade days to black swan and maximum holding period

3. Enter the SPX price

4. Enter the SPX put option strikes and actual ask prices

## Option Valuation

We have entered all of the required input values and are ready to proceed to option valuation. As a result, we will now be concentrating on the right-side of the *EQPutHedge* worksheet, which is depicted in Figure 5.2.

The only user-input required in this section is the maximum implied volatility (IV) value, which is entered in cell E4. The next step in the process is to use the user-supplied market data to solve for the initial or current implied volatilities of the SPX put option candidates.

First, click on the "Clear IVs" push-button macro at the top-left of the *EQPutHedge* worksheet. This will clear the initial implied volatility data (L8:L19), and it will also clear or zero-out the entire right-side of the spreadsheet (M8:S19), because all of these values are derived from the initial implied volatilities of the SPX put option candidates.

After clearing the initial implied volatilities, click on the "Calc IVs" push-button macro at the top-left of the *EQPutHedge* worksheet. This will use the current market-data to calculate the initial implied volatilities for every candidate (L8:L19). To avoid erroneous IV values that usually result from invalid prices, the IV values will be capped at the maximum IV value (E4). If one or more initial IV values (L8:L19) equals the maximum IV value, verify that your pricing data is valid. If it is, consider increasing the maximum IV value (E4).

The *EQPutHedge* worksheet will then automatically repopulate the columns on the right-side of the spreadsheet that are derived from the initial implied volatility values. The initial prices and implied volatilities represent the values at the inception of the hedge. *Projected* implied volatilities are calculated for two distinct future scenarios.

The first scenario assumes *no black-swan event occurs* during the entire holding period of the option strategy (C5). In the "no change" scenario, SPX put options age by the lesser of 1) the actual number of trade days remaining until expiration for each option and 2) the maximum number of trading days specified in cell C5, 33 trade days in this case. In both cases, the initial volatility term structures remain unchanged. The projected "no change" implied volatilities are shown in the cell range M8:M19. The ending "no change" implied volatilities are used to calculate the ending "no change" put option values (O8:O19).

As you would expect, most of the out-of-the-money SPX put options expire worthless, except for a few of the longer-dated options that would still have some remaining time value at the end of 33 trading days. The changes in the option prices from the initial values to the ending "no change" values will be used to calculate the total cost of the hedge per trading day. Since black swan scenarios are rare, the ending "no change" scenario will predominate and we will repeatedly incur these hedging costs.

The second scenario assumes that a black-swan event *does occur* during the holding period, on the trading day specified in cell B5. In the "User change" scenario, the SPX put options age by the number of trading days specified in cell B5, 15 trading days in this case. In the black swan scenario, the shape of the SPX forward term structure remains constant, but the term structure of implied volatilities of SPX put options does not. The changes in the implied volatilities of near-term SPX options are much greater than the changes in implied volatilities of long-term options. The structure of these changes is derived from the VIX futures volatility model, which was introduced in Chapter 4.

The projected "End IV User change" implied volatilities for the black-swan event are shown in the cell range N8:N19. The ending "User change" implied volatilities are used to calculate the ending black swan put option values (P8:P19) after the specified number of trading days in the future (B5).

As intended, all of the SPX put options increase significantly in value. The changes in the option prices from the initial values (K8:K19) to the ending "User change" values (P8:P19) will be used to calculate the hedge profits.

As discussed earlier, the spreadsheet will eventually calculate the effect of the black-swan event on *each* trading day during the holding period. It will loop through every trading day in the holding period to do this calculation – one trading day at a time. As a result, the spreadsheet only depicts the implied volatilities, option values, and hedge profits for a single black-swan event date.

**Parameters**

| | IV/PRC | RF Rt | B/A Spd | | Com/C |
|---|---|---|---|---|---|
| Clear IVs | -1.2400 | 1.00% | 0.10 | | 1.00 |
| Calc IVs | 27.7% | RegT Hedge | MaxIV | | Div Yield |
| | 87.2% | 80.00% | 50.0% | | 1.97% |

HP TDays> 15 | 33 | EQ Index Δ 106,712

| | 5 | 6 | 7 | 8 | 9 | 10 | 11 |
|---|---|---|---|---|---|---|---|
| | 5/19/2017 | 6/16/2017 | 7/21/2017 | 8/18/2017 | 9/15/2017 | 10/20/2017 | 11/17/2017 |
| | 81 | 109 | 144 | 172 | 200 | 235 | 263 |
| | 58 | 77 | 101 | 121 | 140 | 165 | 185 |
| EQ Index Δ | -471.07 | -470.37 | -469.49 | -468.75 | -468.06 | -467.14 | -466.41 |

**Main Table**

| TDTE VIX Δ | TDays | Yrs | EQ Index | Instrument | Initial IV | EndIV NoChg | EndIV UserΔ | Put NoChg | Put UserΔ | User Δ Profit | Avg. Profit | TCost/TD | # Hdg.Trds | Avg % Δ |
|---|---|---|---|---|---|---|---|---|---|---|---|---|---|---|
| 0 | | 0.000 | 2,366.040 | EQ Index | NA | NA | NA | NA | NA | NA | NA | NA | NA | 100.0% |
| 1 | 4 | 0.016 | 2,365.300 | 3/3/2017 | 30.5% | 30.5% | 57.6% | 0.00 | 242.58 | 84,747 | 84,952 | 9.6 | 4 | 89.2% |
| 3 | 9 | 0.036 | 2,364.376 | 3/10/2017 | 26.2% | 30.5% | 50.0% | 0.00 | 209.31 | 83,471 | 84,549 | 13.8 | 2 | 80.4% |
| 13 | 14 | 0.056 | 2,363.452 | 3/17/2017 | 29.5% | 30.5% | 46.3% | 0.00 | 146.64 | 93,320 | 85,452 | 18.7 | 2 | 73.9% |
| 4 | 19 | 0.075 | 2,362.528 | 3/24/2017 | 27.2% | 30.5% | 49.9% | 0.00 | 121.88 | 75,122 | 84,856 | 23.2 | 1 | 68.8% |
| 23 | 38 | 0.151 | 2,359.022 | 4/21/2017 | 22.8% | 29.6% | 35.8% | 0.00 | 150.67 | 87,585 | 85,630 | 39.5 | 1 | 50.9% |
| 43 | 58 | 0.230 | 2,355.336 | 5/19/2017 | 21.4% | 25.8% | 30.8% | 1.29 | 164.39 | 86,058 | 85,380 | 61.0 | 1 | 35.1% |
| 62 | 77 | 0.306 | 2,351.841 | 6/16/2017 | 21.2% | 22.4% | 28.9% | 3.14 | 176.69 | 85,437 | 84,947 | 93.2 | 1 | 28.4% |
| 86 | 101 | 0.401 | 2,347.432 | 7/21/2017 | 21.4% | 21.3% | 28.0% | 7.39 | 191.96 | 86,261 | 85,844 | 126.7 | 1 | 24.3% |
| 106 | 121 | 0.480 | 2,343.765 | 8/18/2017 | | | | | | 0 | 0 | | 1 | 22.3% |
| 125 | 140 | 0.556 | 2,340.286 | 9/15/2017 | | | | | | 0 | 0 | | 1 | 20.9% |
| 150 | 165 | 0.655 | 2,335.717 | 10/20/2017 | | | | | | 0 | 0 | | 1 | 19.5% |
| 170 | 185 | 0.734 | 2,332.068 | 11/17/2017 | | | | | | 0 | 0 | | 1 | 18.5% |

Figure 5.2: SPX Put Hedge (RHS)

Terms | Holidays | PositionSize | FutureHedge | VIXCallHedge | EQPutHedge | EQPutHedge

The *EQPutHedge* worksheet will use the hedge profits in conjunction with the hedge objective to determine the required number of SPX put option contracts to purchase for each candidate. The number of required contracts (the hedge solution) is required to calculate the average profits and the total costs per day of each hedge. We will review the procedure required to generate the hedge solutions in the next section.

## Hedge Solution

This section will reference the left-side (Figure 5.1), right-side (Figure 5.2), and bottom-left section (Figure 5.3) of the *EQPutHedge* worksheet. After calculating the ending implied volatilities and option values for the "no change" and "User change" scenarios in the previous section, we only need one additional set of values to complete the remaining *EQPutHedge* spreadsheet calculations: the number of SPX put option contracts required (I8:I19 in Figure 5.1).

There is only one additional user input value required in this section. The *EQPutHedge* spreadsheet can calculate the hedge solutions based on the black swan scenario profits on a *single scenario event date* (B5) or on the *average black swan scenario profits* over every date in the holding period (C5). The *profit type* user-variable is entered in a drop-down box in cell E23 (Figure 5.3). The *"Scenario"* option uses the profit from the single scenario date (B5) and the *"Average"* option uses the average black swan profits over every date in the holding period (C5). Users will typically solve for hedge solutions using the *average* black swan profit over all holding period dates.

As explained in Chapter 4, the spreadsheet needs a set of sample hedge solutions (number of put option contracts) in order to calculate and re-calibrate the average profit values. You could enter a set of sample hedge values by hand, but I created a macro that automatically populates the cells I8:I19 (Figure 5.1) with sample solution values of ten contracts.

To populate these cells, click on the push-button macro "Populate Sample Hedge Values" (Figure 5.3). This macro will also zero-out the average profit values (R8:R19 in Figure 5.2), because the spreadsheet recognizes that the average profit values are dependent on the hedge solution values (I8:I19 in Figure 5.1). The macro will also clear the profit values in cells W8:Z19 (not shown). Since we changed the number of contracts, the old average profit values are no longer valid.

Before calculating the actual number of contracts required, we must recalculate the average black swan profit values (R8:R19 in Figure 5.2) for the sample number of contracts (I8:I19 in Figure 5.1). Click on the "Calc Average User Change Profit" (Figure 5.3) push-button macro to calculate the average black swan profit. The macro will calculate the black swan scenario profit for every trading day in the holding period and then calculate the average of these values. The new average profit values will be saved in cells R8:R19 (Figure 5.2).

We are finally ready to calculate the *actual* hedge solutions based on the *average* black swan profits for the entire holding period. Select *"Average"* from the drop down list in cell E23 (Figure 5.3) and then click on the "Calc Hedge NP" (Figure 5.3) push-button macro. This will calculate the number of put contracts (I8:I19 in Figure 5.1) required to satisfy the hedge objective (D4:D5) based on the average black swan profits (R8:R19 in Figure 5.2) over the entire holding period (C5).

As you might have guessed, since we changed the number of contracts, the macro cleared the average profit values again. Rerun the "Calc Average User Change Profit" macro (Figure 5.3) to calculate the revised average black swan profit values. Now all of the spreadsheet cells will be populated for each of the put option candidates.

Note that the re-calculated average black swan profit values (R8:R19 in Figure 5.2) range from $84,947 to $85,884, which are very close to the hedge profit objective of $85,370 (106,712 X 80%). The average profit variation is due to rounding the number of contracts to the first decimal place. Rounding has a greater impact in this spreadsheet due to the fewer number of option contracts required to hedge (relative to the *VIXCallHedge* worksheet).

Before examining the individual hedge solutions, I want to emphasize again that you can also manually round the number of contracts to the nearest whole number before re-calculating the average black swan profit values. I intentionally *did not* round these values in this article, because I wanted to make the final solutions as intuitive as possible. In addition, I wanted to illustrate that the hedge solutions would all satisfy the specified hedge profit objective. In practice, rounded values are required to accurately calculate hedge costs and profits.

Below is a review of the steps required to calculate the hedge solution based on the average black swan profit (Figure 5.3):

1. Click on the "Populate Sample Hedge Values" button,
2. Click on the "Calc Average User Change Profit" button,
3. Select "Average" from the drop-down list (E23),
4. Click on the "Calc Hedge NP" button, and
5. Click on the "Calc Average User Change Profit" button.

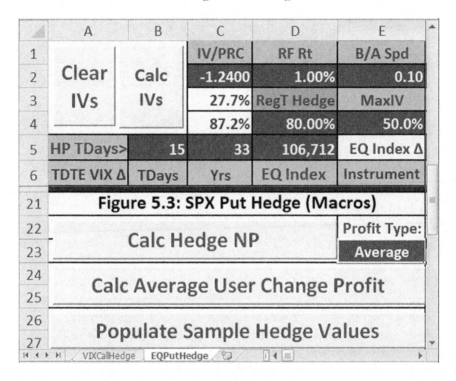

The goal of this chapter is to identify the most efficient *SPX put option hedge* to mitigate the risk of random catastrophic events. The SPX put option with the lowest total cost per trade day (S8:S19 in Figure 5.2) is the most efficient hedging solution. The SPX put option hedge solution with the lowest cost per trade day (including slippage and commissions) requires the purchase of 3.5 SPX put options with an expiration date of 3/3/2017 and a strike price of $2,135 (line 8: Figure 5.1 & Figure 5.2). The total calculated hedging cost per day (including slippage and commissions) is only $9.6. Note that the total hedging cost per day would increase to $11.0 when rounding the number of put option contracts from 3.5 to 4.0 (not shown).

Since the 3/3/2017 put option expires in only four trading days, the hedge solution also assumes that this same option (with four trading days remaining until expiration) would be repurchased repeatedly during the option strategy holding period to maintain the desired level of catastrophic risk protection.

The cumulative cost of maintaining the lowest cost hedge solution over the entire 33 trading-day holding period would be $363 ($11.0 per trading day X 33 trading days). This would reduce the profitability of each iron condor trade by only 0.34% ($363 / $106,712). This represents a significant savings relative to the lowest cost VIX call hedging solution of $726 ($22 per trading day X 33 trading days) or 0.68% ($726 / $106,712).

As we saw in the VIX call hedging solution, the total cost per day varies significantly, from a low of $9.6 per trading day to a high of $126.7 per trading day. The cost range is not as wide as in the VIX call hedging example, but choosing the wrong put option hedging candidate would be expensive and could compromise the profitability of the option strategy.

## Scenario Analysis

In the previous section, we solved for the number of put option contracts required to meet our hedge profit objective based on the average profit. The "Calc Average User Change Profit" macro (Figure 5.3) calculates the average profit, minimum profit, maximum profit, and profit range for black-swan events occurring over the entire range of trading days in the holding period. These values are provided in cells W8:Z19 of the *EQPutHedge* worksheet (not shown).

I compiled these results in Figure 5.4, along with the total hedge cost per day that we calculated in the previous section. As you will recall, the SPX put option hedge solution with the lowest cost per trade day (including slippage and commissions) requires the purchase of 3.5 SPX put options with an expiration date of 3/3/2017 and a strike price of $2,135.

## Figure 5.4: SPX Put Hedge, Scenario Profits for Events on Trade Days 0 - 33

| Instrument | Hedge NP | Put Strike | TCost/TD | Avg. Profit | Min Profit | Max Profit | Profit Range |
|---|---|---|---|---|---|---|---|
| EQ Index | NA | NA | NA | NA | NA | NA | NA |
| 3/3/2017 | 3.5 | 2135.00 | 9.6 | 84,952 | 84,593 | 85,445 | 852 |
| 3/10/2017 | 4.0 | 2100.00 | 13.8 | 84,549 | 82,957 | 86,572 | 3,614 |
| 3/17/2017 | 6.4 | 2000.00 | 18.7 | 85,452 | 70,361 | 94,793 | 24,432 |
| 3/24/2017 | 6.2 | 2000.00 | 23.2 | 84,856 | 68,471 | 94,327 | 25,856 |
| 4/21/2017 | 5.9 | 2000.00 | 39.5 | 85,630 | 71,872 | 94,778 | 22,907 |
| 5/19/2017 | 5.4 | 2000.00 | 61.0 | 85,380 | 79,206 | 90,898 | 11,692 |
| 6/16/2017 | 5.1 | 2000.00 | 93.2 | 84,947 | 80,126 | 89,517 | 9,391 |
| 7/21/2017 | 4.9 | 2000.00 | 126.7 | 85,844 | 81,707 | 89,793 | 8,086 |
| 8/18/2017 | -2.0 | NA | NA | NA | NA | NA | NA |
| 9/15/2017 | -1.0 | NA | NA | NA | NA | NA | NA |
| 10/20/2017 | 0.0 | NA | NA | NA | NA | NA | NA |
| 11/17/2017 | 0.0 | NA | NA | NA | NA | NA | NA |

The average, minimum, and maximum hedge profits for the lowest cost hedge are $84,952, $84,593, and $85,445, respectively. The resulting max-min range was only $852. The resulting range was much lower than the range of the lowest cost VIX call hedge ($30,762 in Figure 4.6). The relative volatility differences of the VIX futures contracts significantly increase the profit variability of the VIX call hedge solutions.

The next lowest cost solution was the SPX put option with an expiration date of 3/10/2017 and a strike price of $2,100. The total cost per day was approximately 44% higher than the lowest cost solution ($13.8 versus $9.6) and the profit range was almost 325% higher ($3,614 versus $852). The lowest cost SPX put solution also had the narrowest profit range (least risk). I suggest reviewing the average profit, minimum profit, maximum profit, and the profit range when deciding on your desired hedge candidate.

Now that we have solved for the hedge solutions for each SPX put option candidate, we can also use the *EQPutHedge* worksheet as a scenario analysis tool. We originally assumed that SPX would decrease by 20% in response to a discrete catastrophic event. The hedge solutions were derived from this SPX forecast. We can now examine how our hedge would perform if SPX were to decrease by a different percentage amount.

The left-side of Figure 5.5 describes each SPX put option candidate solution: expiration date, number of contracts, strike price, and total hedge cost per trading day. The right side of Figure 5.5 shows the average profit for several SPX scenarios: SPX-10%, SPX-15%, SPX-20%, SPX-25%, SPX-30%, and the average over all scenarios. To calculate the average hedge profits for each scenario, enter the desired change in SPX in cell F5 of the *EQPutHedge* worksheet and then click on the "Calc Average User Change Profit" (Figure 5.3) push-button macro. The macro will calculate the new average profit, minimum profit, maximum profit, and profit range for the new SPX scenario.

Note that we did not change the hedge solution. We are using the scenario analysis tool to evaluate how our proposed hedge solution would perform in different SPX environments. As we would expect, the hedge solutions generated much lower average profits in the SPX-10% and SPX-15% scenarios.

## Figure 5.5: SPX Put Hedge, Average Profits for VIX Change Scenarios

| Instrument | Hedge NP | Put Strike | TCost/TD | SPX - 10% | SPX - 15% | SPX - 20% | SPX - 25% | SPX - 30% | Avg. ALL |
|---|---|---|---|---|---|---|---|---|---|
| EQ Index | NA | NA | NA | NA | NA | NA | NA | NA | NA |
| 3/3/2017 | 3.5 | 2135.00 | 9.6 | 13,085 | 45,167 | 84,952 | 126,103 | 167,460 | 87,353 |
| 3/10/2017 | 4.0 | 2100.00 | 13.8 | 11,596 | 42,066 | 84,549 | 130,601 | 177,574 | 89,277 |
| 3/17/2017 | 6.4 | 2000.00 | 18.7 | 8,665 | 34,911 | 85,452 | 150,877 | 222,581 | 100,497 |
| 3/24/2017 | 6.2 | 2000.00 | 23.2 | 9,621 | 36,241 | 84,856 | 147,387 | 216,271 | 98,875 |
| 4/21/2017 | 5.9 | 2000.00 | 39.5 | 12,499 | 40,081 | 85,630 | 143,383 | 207,565 | 97,832 |
| 5/19/2017 | 5.4 | 2000.00 | 61.0 | 17,780 | 45,109 | 85,380 | 135,520 | 191,958 | 95,149 |
| 6/16/2017 | 5.1 | 2000.00 | 93.2 | 21,087 | 47,716 | 84,947 | 130,717 | 182,437 | 93,381 |
| 7/21/2017 | 4.9 | 2000.00 | 126.7 | 24,474 | 50,756 | 85,844 | 128,334 | 176,372 | 93,156 |
| 8/18/2017 | -2.0 | NA | NA | NA | NA | NA | NA | NA | NA |
| 9/15/2017 | -1.0 | NA | NA | NA | NA | NA | NA | NA | NA |
| 10/20/2017 | 0.0 | NA | NA | NA | NA | NA | NA | NA | NA |
| 11/17/2017 | 0.0 | NA | NA | NA | NA | NA | NA | NA | NA |

However, in these scenarios, the iron condor losses might not have been as extreme. This tool should be used in conjunction with your options analytical platform to evaluate the combined position.

For the SPX-25% and SPX-30% scenarios, the average hedge profits would have increased significantly - enough to guarantee a profit for the aggregate position, even after losing 100% of the required capital on the iron condor. We saw the same behavior in the VIX call hedge solutions.

Several of the other SPX put option candidates offer higher average hedge profits across all five SPX black swan scenarios, but that is not our principal concern. Instead, we should focus on the scenarios that generate the lowest hedge profits: SPX-10% and SPX-15%. The 3/3/2017 SPX put option outperforms the other low cost put candidates in both of these scenarios. In other words, it offers more protection or higher hedge profits at a lower cost. Finally, the 3/3/2017 option also had a much narrower profit range over all trading days than all of the other SPX put option candidates (Figure 5.4).

## Summary

I hope this second option hedging example helped you become more familiar with the option hedging tools in the OSHRM spreadsheet.

In summary, there are six principal components of the *EQPutHedge* spreadsheet:
1. Hedge Objective,
2. Catastrophic Risk Event,
3. Market Data,
4. Option Valuation,
5. Hedge Solution, and
6. Scenario Analysis

As I explained in the last chapter, the best way to become proficient with the spreadsheet is to experiment. Begin with the original data set before moving on to real-time market data. Study the interaction of the variables by varying the input values. The spreadsheet is both an educational device and a practical tool that can complement your investment process.

# 6 - PRACTICAL CONSIDERATIONS

In this final chapter, I would like to attempt to answer a few lingering questions about applying the hedging techniques in practice.

**Q. Can the spreadsheet hedging tools be applied to other underlying securities?**

**A.** Yes. SPX, NDX, and RUT are the easiest underlying securities to hedge, because they each have their own specific futures contract. SPX, NDX, and RUT put options are also sufficiently liquid to use for hedging catastrophic events.

However, VIX options are currently the only liquid volatility option vehicle. The VIX index is derived from SPX options, but that does not mean that VIX call options could not be used to hedge RUT and NDX option strategies. If the SPX declines by 20%, I can guarantee that the RUT and NDX will suffer similar extreme moves. The spreadsheet tools can also be applied to option strategies based on individual stocks or even futures. That said, VIX call options cannot be used to hedge company-specific catastrophic events.

**Q. Can the spreadsheet hedging tools be applied to different option strategies?**

**A.** Of course. The hedging procedure is exactly the same. Using your options analytical platform, solve for the position Delta of the specific option strategy at the exit trigger points and use the *FuturesHedge* tool to solve for the required number of futures contracts to buy and sell.

## Q. What type of positions should I hedge?

**A.** Any position that is negatively exposed to an increase in realized volatility (negative Gamma) or an increase in implied volatility (negative Vega). Option strategies with negative Gamma incur losses at a faster and faster rate in response to price changes in the underlying security. Option strategies with negative Vega are adversely affected by increases in implied volatility.

To make matters worse, many option income strategies have both negative Gamma *and* negative Vega. In addition, increased realized volatility often generates increases in implied volatility. When a catastrophic event occurs, the combined effects of Gamma and Vega can be devastating to unhedged traders.

Surprisingly, options are not the only type of instrument that is exposed to changes in volatility. There are now several exchange traded notes (ETNs) or exchange traded funds (ETFs) that are effectively short volatility. XIV and SVSY are two of the most liquid inverse volatility funds.

Should they be hedged as well? Absolutely. I have several algorithmic strategies that trade volatility ETNs and they all have a maximum stop amount of approximately 10%. If a catastrophic event occurred while holding an inverse ETN like XIV, its value could drop to zero overnight. Fortunately, these types of strategies generate very high returns on required capital, so they could easily absorb the incremental costs of the catastrophic risk hedge.

Using the above rule-of-thumb, any position that is negatively exposed to an increase in realized volatility (negative Gamma) or an increase in implied volatility (negative Vega) should be hedged; this includes inverse volatility derivatives.

## Q. When do I hedge?

**A.** Any time you have an open position that is negatively exposed to an increase in realized volatility (negative Gamma) or an increase in implied volatility (negative Vega). The stop limit or conditional futures orders should be placed as soon as practicable after entering the trade. Enter the trade into your options analytical platform, model the Delta exposure for the up and down exit scenarios, and solve for the required number of contracts to buy and sell.

Similarly, as soon as the short Gamma position is entered, solve for the most efficient hedge based on current market prices, and purchase the required number of VIX call or underlying put options to satisfy your hedging objective. Black-swan events can happen at any time.

When you close a negative Gamma position, sell any remaining long VIX call or long underlying put options - if any time value remains. If not, there is no risk in holding "worthless" long out-of-the money options. If a catastrophic event *does occur* before the options expire, take your unexpected windfall and buy your neighbor's beach house for pennies on the dollar.

## Q. Should I hedge with futures or options?

**A.** Both – belt and suspenders. There is no guarantee that the futures order will fill in the event of a discrete catastrophic event. The market could be closed at the time of the event. In addition, the futures order is designed to hedge the position Delta risk of your strategy at the target exit levels.

The long option hedges are designed to protect against black swan type events. Once you purchase the option, you will retain the catastrophic risk protection until it expires.

## Q. Should I use VIX call options or underlying put options?

**A.** Whichever offers the lowest cost, lowest risk solution for your particular black swan scenario, based on actual real-time prices. The analytical framework and spreadsheet tools are designed to be applicable to different environments. Market prices vary over time, as will the optimal hedging solutions.

If the cost of VIX call and underlying put options is similar, you could use a combination of both techniques to hedge your black swan risk. This would partially diversify your model risk, which is a function of your price and volatility assumptions.

## Q. Will the spreadsheet hedge values be precise if a black-swan event occurs?

**A.** Precise – no, plausible – yes. There is no model that could correctly predict option prices in the event of a discrete 45-point increase in the VIX or a 20% decline in SPX. However, the analytical framework, volatility risk model, and the implied volatility / SPX beta were all derived from actual market prices and actual market environments. I use these models in my own trading.

While it is impossible to precisely predict option values in advance, well-designed models can be used to determine realistic values, which can be used to make prudent hedging decisions. This is especially true if these types of tools are used repeatedly to evaluate different scenarios with a range of input assumptions.

## Conclusion

My goal in writing this article was to describe how practical hedging and risk management techniques can be applied to option strategies, and to provide tools that would be accessible to motivated option traders.

I hope you found the position sizing, futures hedging, VIX call hedging, and underlying put hedging techniques and tools to be both useful and educational. I encourage you to use these same tools and techniques to enhance your own research and to compliment your existing investment process.

\* \* \*

Please see the Resources Chapter at the end of this article for a description of reader discounts available on the products and services I personally use in my proprietary trading and research. In addition, the Resources Chapter also has information on how to download the OSHRM spreadsheet that accompanies this article.

# ABOUT THE AUTHOR

Brian Johnson designed, programmed, and implemented the first return sensitivity based parametric framework actively used to control risk in fixed income portfolios. He further extended the capabilities of this approach by designing and programming an integrated series of option valuation, prepayment, and portfolio optimization models.

Based on this technology, Mr. Johnson founded Lincoln Capital Management's fixed income index business, where he ultimately managed over $13 billion in assets for some of the largest and most sophisticated institutional clients in the U.S. and around the globe.

He later served as the President of a financial consulting and software development firm, designing artificial intelligence-based forecasting and risk management systems for institutional investment managers.

Mr. Johnson is now a full-time proprietary trader in options, futures, stocks, and ETFs primarily using algorithmic trading strategies. In addition to his professional investment experience, he also designed and taught courses in financial derivatives for MBA, Masters of Accounting, and undergraduate business programs - most recently as a Professor of Practice at the University of North Carolina's Kenan-Flagler Business School.

He is the author of three groundbreaking books on options: 1) *Option Strategy Risk / Return Ratios: A Revolutionary New Approach to Optimizing, Adjusting, and Trading Any Option Income Strategy*, 2) *Exploiting Earnings Volatility: An Innovative New Approach to Evaluating, Optimizing, and Trading Option Strategies to Profit from Earnings Announcements*, and 3) *Trading Option Volatility: A Breakthrough in Option Valuation, Yielding Practical Insights into Strategy Design, Simulation, Optimization, Risk Management, and Profits.*

He recently authored two in-depth (100+ page) articles on option strategy. The first, *Option Income Strategy Trade Filters,* represents the culmination of years of research into developing a systematic framework for optimizing the timing of Option Income Strategy (OIS) trades. The second, *Option Strategy Hedging and Risk Management*, presents a comprehensive analytical framework and accompanying spreadsheet tools for managing and hedging option strategy risk in real-world market environments.

He has also written articles for the *Financial Analysts Journal*, *Active Trader*, and *Seeking Alpha* and he regularly shares his trading insights and research ideas as the editor of https://www.traderedge.net/.

Mr. Johnson holds a B.S. degree in Finance with high honors from the University of Illinois at Urbana-Champaign and an MBA degree with a specialization in Finance from the University of Chicago Booth School of Business.

Email: BJohnson@TraderEdge.Net

# RESOURCES

I write a wide range of free, informative articles on https://www.traderedge.net/. The goal of Trader Edge is to provide information and ideas that will help you enhance your investment process and improve your trading results. The articles cover many different topics: economic indicators, technical analysis, market commentary, options, futures, stocks, exchange traded funds (ETFs), strategy development, trade analysis, and risk management. You will find educational articles that appeal to the beginner, as well as advanced tools and strategies to support more experienced traders. I have also created several instructional spreadsheet videos, which are associated with my books and articles: https://traderedge.net/category/video/

## Brian Johnson's Books & Articles

*Option Strategy Risk / Return Ratios: A Revolutionary New Approach to Optimizing, Adjusting, and Trading Any Option Income Strategy*

For the first time, the pivotal concepts of risk and return have been integrated into a consistent approach for managing option income strategies. The risk/return ratios introduced in this book will allow you to evaluate, compare, adjust, and even optimize any option income strategy, on any underlying security, in any market environment. The accompanying Excel spreadsheet will allow every trader to integrate these new tools into their investment process.

*Exploiting Earnings Volatility: An Innovative New Approach to Evaluating, Optimizing, and Trading Option Strategies to Profit from Earnings Announcements*

The analytical framework introduced in this book will allow you to evaluate, compare, and even optimize option earning strategies on any underlying security, in any market environment. The accompanying Excel spreadsheets will help every trader integrate these new tools into their investment process. The spreadsheets include a comprehensive volatility model and a strategy optimizer. The toolset even calculates "True Greeks," including a new Greek risk metric designed specifically for earnings strategies.

## *Option Income Strategy Trade Filters: An In-Depth Article Demonstrating the Use of Trade Filters to Enhance Returns and Reduce Risk.*

*Option Income Strategy Trade Filters*, represents the culmination of years of research into developing a systematic framework for optimizing the timing of Option Income Strategy (OIS) trades. The research was based on the analysis of 15,434 OIS trades, each with a comprehensive set of objective, tradable entry and exit rules. The OIS strategy back-test results for ten different types of filters are evaluated in this article, including unique filter combinations that delivered exceptional results. The results of over 100 different back-tests are provided.

## *Trading Option Volatility: A Breakthrough in Option Valuation - Yielding Practical Insights into Strategy Design, Simulation, Optimization, Risk Management, and Profits*

Trading Option Volatility represents a breakthrough in option valuation, which has profound implications for option strategy design, option and volatility trading, and even for calculating accurate and reliable option risk metrics (Greeks). Brian Johnson has developed a practical new analytical framework that eliminates the invalid constant volatility and interest rate assumptions of conventional models, and generates theoretically correct and internally consistent, current and future option prices, volatility index futures prices, and risk metrics (Greeks), across all term structures of volatilities and all term structures of interest rates - providing an exploitable edge for option traders.

# OIS Universal Filter Subscription

Trading Insights, LLC offers a monthly subscription to the proprietary Option Income Strategy Universal Filter (OISUF) algorithm, which I introduced in my recent article *Option Income Strategy Trade Filters: An In-Depth Article Demonstrating the Use of Trade Filters to Enhance Returns and Reduce Risk*. The OISUF algorithm calculates a real-time, standardized option income strategy (OIS) score that quantitatively differentiates among the entire spectrum of favorable and unfavorable OIS environments. The OISUF algorithm is run via macros on an Excel spreadsheet, which requires a one-time download.

The spreadsheet is simple to use and has built-in macros to import free (as of this writing) Yahoo (price) and CBOE (IV) data. Data from alternative sources can also be copied and pasted as desired. The OISUF may be applied to options on any underlying security that has a corresponding volatility index. An explanation of the OISUF follows, but a more detailed description of the OISUF is available via this link: https://traderedge.net/order/ois-universal-filter/. Please see the *Option Income Strategy Trade Filters* article for the most comprehensive discussion of the OISUF.

The published performance results were based on the analysis of 15,434 iron condor trades, each with a comprehensive set of objective, tradable entry and exit rules. The results for each of the 15,000 plus trades were scaled to a constant dollar amount at risk, to ensure all trades were equally-weighted when calculating the performance metrics. I ran the back-tests using end-of-day data on options with monthly expiration dates from May 2004 to May 2016. The back-test results were all based on actual option prices.

The OIS Universal Filter (OISUF) is a standardized metric calculated by an algorithm that exclusively uses historical and current prices and implied volatilities. The volatility index is used as a proxy for implied volatility, which limits the application of the OISUF to underlying securities that have corresponding volatility indices.

The OISUF algorithm has very few parameters. It captures the fundamental relationships between price, implied volatility, and OIS performance. It was not derived from a specific dataset and the *parameters were not optimized*. As a result, the *parameters in the algorithm will never change and will never be re-estimated*. The limited number of non-optimized parameters greatly enhances the robustness of the OISUF.

The parameter values were structural and were chosen before strategy testing. Structural means the OISUF parameter values were a byproduct of the market-edge hypothesis itself. They were the only parameter values tested. Despite the use of structural, pre-determined parameter values, the OISUF algorithm is very responsive to changing market conditions. It can be used to systematically quantify the attractiveness of OIS trade entry environments in real time.

I call it the OIS Universal Filter because it can be applied to enhance the risk-adjusted returns of option income strategies almost universally. It is applicable to any Delta-neutral option income strategy that does not require time (calendar) spread components.

The OIS Universal Filter algorithm produces a standardized OIS score. In this context, the word "standardized" means the resulting OIS scores are directly comparable across all underlying securities. OIS scores are not bounded, but typically fall between negative 200 and positive 100.

Scores below zero indicate unfavorable OIS environments and scores above zero signify favorable OIS environments. Furthermore, higher OIS scores imply more advantageous OIS environments across the entire spectrum of prospective OIS values.

Below is a brief overview of the OISUF performance metrics in Figure R.1. A much more comprehensive explanation is available in the article *Option Income Strategy Trade Filters*. The first two columns on the left-side of Figure R.1 describe the OISUF condition. The next three columns show the performance metrics (profit factor, percentage of winning trades, and average return on margin) for each filter condition. The final column documents the percentage of the 15,434 managed iron condor trades that met the OISUF conditions.

All three performance metrics were an increasing function of the OIS scores across the entire spectrum of OIS score thresholds. In fact, there was only a single case when the performance metrics did not increase for a corresponding increase in OIS score. Despite this minor inconsistency, the OIS score threshold and the performance metrics were almost perfectly positively correlated.

The OISUF algorithm was able to objectively differentiate among favorable and unfavorable OIS trading environments across the entire spectrum of OIS scores. More information about the OISUF subscription is available via the following link:

114

https://traderedge.net/order/ois-universal-filter/.

| Figure R.1: 1TPS - OIS Filter (RUT, SPX, NDX) | | | | | |
|---|---|---|---|---|---|
| OIS Condition | OIS Score Threshold | Profit Factor | % Winning Trades | Avg. Return on Margin | % of Total Trades |
| N/A (ALL) | N/A (ALL) | 2.10 | 85.10% | 3.22% | 100.00% |
| OIS Score <= | -200 | 0.63 | 61.72% | -3.67% | 0.83% |
| OIS Score <= | -180 | 0.70 | 64.25% | -2.87% | 1.25% |
| OIS Score <= | -160 | 0.77 | 66.53% | -1.99% | 1.53% |
| OIS Score <= | -140 | 0.84 | 68.66% | -1.34% | 1.84% |
| OIS Score <= | -120 | 0.89 | 70.18% | -0.83% | 2.22% |
| OIS Score <= | -100 | 1.16 | 75.32% | 0.99% | 3.07% |
| OIS Score <= | -80 | 1.25 | 77.01% | 1.40% | 4.20% |
| OIS Score <= | -60 | 1.47 | 80.30% | 2.19% | 6.97% |
| OIS Score <= | -40 | 1.65 | 82.58% | 2.57% | 13.54% |
| OIS Score <= | -20 | 1.98 | 84.89% | 3.16% | 27.18% |
| OIS Score >= | 0 | 2.29 | 85.86% | 3.46% | 49.59% |
| OIS Score >= | 20 | 2.80 | 87.78% | 4.10% | 25.14% |
| OIS Score >= | 40 | 5.15 | 92.89% | 5.53% | 11.12% |
| OIS Score >= | 60 | 7.52 | 95.32% | 6.34% | 4.15% |
| OIS Score >= | 80 | 6.01 | 94.27% | 6.45% | 1.24% |
| OIS Score >= | 100 | 20.69 | 98.36% | 8.13% | 0.40% |
| OIS Score Correlation | | N/A | 0.996 | 0.994 | N/A |

## AI Volatility Edge (AIVE) Subscription

Trading Insights, LLC offers a monthly subscription to the proprietary AI Volatility Edge platform, which I mentioned several times in this book. The AI Volatility Edge (AIVE) platform aggregates the results from 360 separate AI / Machine-learning models to forecast: four different volatility measures, for three different equity indices (SPX, NDX, and RUT), for 13 future time periods (5, 10, 15, 21, 31, 42, 63, 84, 105, 126, 189, 252, and 504 trade days).

The algorithm also interpolates or extrapolates as required to calculate volatility forecasts for any specific option expiration date in the future. The AI Volatility Edge platform can calculate volatility estimates based on end-of-day (EOD) historical data, current EOD data, or even based on the latest real-time (intra-day) price and volatility data.

The AI Volatility Edge platform forecasts four different volatility measures that are essential for the option trader: *future realized volatility, future realized terminal volatility, future realized extreme volatility, and the modeled value of volatility index itself* (VIX, VXN, or RVX). *Future realized volatility* represents the expected annualized root mean square of the log of the future daily equity index returns. That sounds complicated, but the important point is that the resulting forecasts are directly comparable to both ATM implied volatility for the equity index options and the corresponding volatility index.

The *future realized terminal volatility* is not annualized and represents the expected continuously compounded percentage price change (plus or minus) of the equity index from the forecast date *until the end of the forecast period*. In other words, it is the *magnitude of expected price change*. The *future realized extreme volatility* is similar and is also not annualized. It represents the *maximum interim* expected continuously compounded percentage price change (plus or minus) experienced by the equity index *at any time* between the forecast date and the end of the forecast period. Said differently, it is the *maximum expected price change*. Both of these values are extremely useful when evaluating alternative strike prices and determining prospective adjustment points for all option strategies.

The final volatility estimate is of the volatility index itself. We obviously know the value of the volatility index, but that value may be unusually high or low relative to the AI model's algorithmic evaluation of the recent price and volatility history.

This is the purpose of the platform: *to utilize the latest in AI technology to forecast, identify, and quantify anomalies between the AI expected future volatilities and the entire term structure of volatilities expected by the market (priced into index options and volatility index futures).*

The AI Volatility Edge platform is delivered via three separate Excel spreadsheets, one for each equity index (SPX, NDX, and RUT). The volatility forecasts are run via macros on Excel spreadsheets, which requires a one-time download.

The platform is simple to use and has built-in push-button macros to import free (as of this writing) Yahoo (price) and CBOE (IV) data. In addition, the platform also provides alternative push-button macros to import data from daily files provided by the third-party vendor Commodity Systems Inc. (CSI). Please see the CSI section later in this Resources Chapter for more information.

Data from alternative sources can also be copied and pasted as desired. A more detailed description of the AI Volatility Edge Platform and monthly subscription is available via this link: https://traderedge.net/order/ai-volatility-edge/. The link is also accessible in the RHS side-bar of the TraderEdge.Net site.

## OptionVue

Through our referral agreement, OptionVue is offering an exclusive 15% discount on the initial purchase of any *annual* subscription of any OptionVue product and on all Discover Options educational products. However, the discount is not available to current OptionVue clients with an active OptionVue subscription. Please use the coupon code "traderedge" (*lower case with no spaces or quotation marks*) to receive your 15% discount when ordering applicable products from OptionVue online or over the phone.

I encourage you to visit http://www.optionvue.com/traderedge.html and take advantage of the exclusive 15% Trader Edge referral discount. If you would prefer to evaluate the OptionVue software before placing an order, the above link will also allow you to enroll in a free 30-day trial of OptionVue's option analytical platform. This link is also available in the RHS sidebar of the TraderEdge.Net site.

Trading options without a comprehensive option analytical platform is not advisable and the OptionVue software is one of the most powerful tools available. Unlike most broker platforms, OptionVue evaluates both the horizontal and vertical volatility skews, resulting in much more realistic calculations and more accurate risk and valuation metrics. In addition, I worked with OptionVue to help them apply the aggregate implied volatility formula to quantify the effects of earnings volatility before and after earnings events in the OptionVue software.

The OptionVue software also includes a very powerful "Trade Finder" module, which is similar to the strategy optimization tool in the *Exploiting Earnings Volatility* Integrated spreadsheet. Trade Finder allows the user to specify an objective, strategy candidates, filters, and forecast adjustments and uses those inputs to search for the best possible strategy. Most important, *Trade Finder uses the aggregate implied volatility formula to accurately incorporate the effects of earnings volatility in its analysis.*

OptionVue also offers a subscription service specifically designed for "Earnings Plays." OptionVue's description of the five Earnings Play's strategies follows:

- Prime Movers: Stocks that make big moves - options tend to be undervalued.

-   Prime Non-Movers: Stocks that make smaller-than-expected moves, options tend to be overvalued.

- Earnings Pairs: Two stocks in the same industry, only one of which is announcing earnings.

- Echoes - Two stocks in the same industry, with one announcing 1-18 days after the other.

- Runners - Stocks that tend to run in price after the earnings announcement.

This system is based on the hypothetical results actual trades would have experienced in the past and shows you a quality ranking for each trade along with its past success rate.

OptionVue offers real-time and historical option prices, which can be used to back-test option strategies, even with adjustments. OptionVue also offers subscriptions to proprietary strategies, including their VXX Trading System.

Finally, Discover Options, the educational arm of OptionVue, offers one-on-one personal option mentoring from professional option traders with decades of experience.

## OptionSlam.com

During the course of my research for my second book (*Exploiting Earnings Volatility*), I collaborated with the owners of OptionSlam.com on several enhancements for their site that will help all traders who use option strategies to trade earnings announcements.

Given the strong synergies between OptionSlam.com and the tools in my second book, OptionSlam.com has agreed to offer an exclusive 15% discount on annual INSIDER Memberships to my readers.

The following benefits are provided to all INSIDER OptionSlam.com Members:
- View Earnings History of Individual Stocks
- View Volatility History of Individual Stocks
- View Straddle Tracking History of Individual Stocks
- View and Customize the Upcoming Earnings Filter
- View and Customize the Earnings Calendar
- View Weekly Implied Volatility Report
- View and Customize the Best Trending Stocks Report
- View and Customize the Current Monthly and Weekly Straddles Report
- View and Customize the Historical Straddles Report
- View Trades from All Members
- Customize and Schedule Email Alerts of Personalized Reports
- Export Earnings Statistics to Excel


OptionSlam.com's historical earnings data provides all of the return and volatility data necessary to evaluate past earnings performance. The "Upcoming Earnings Filter" is a powerful and flexible tool that will help you efficiently identify both directional and non-directional trading candidates.

I encourage you to visit https://www.optionslam.com/partner_info/traderedge and take advantage of the exclusive 15% Trader Edge referral discount. Note underscore ("_") between "partner" and "info" in above link. The Option Slam link is also available in the RHS side-bar of the TraderEdge.Net site. You may also contact OptionVue via phone (847-816-6610) and ask for the Trader Edge discount.

## CSI

Reliable prices are essential for developing and implementing systematic trading strategies. Commodity Systems Inc. (CSI) is one of the leading providers of market data and trading software for institutional and retail customers. Please use the CSI link in the RHS sidebar of the TraderEdge.Net site to learn more about CSI's pricing subscriptions.

## Affiliate Relationships

I am a customer of OptionSlam, OptionVue and CSI. Trading Insights, LLC, also has an affiliate referral relationship with OptionSlam.com, OptionVue, and CSI.

## OSHRM Spreadsheet Tools

Purchasing this book entitles you to an individual user license to download and use the associated risk/return Excel spreadsheets for your own research. However, you may not transfer or share the copyrighted spreadsheet, passwords, or download links with others.

There is a single Excel spreadsheet that accompanies this article. The name of the spreadsheet is OSHRM.xlsm. The use of the spreadsheet was explained throughout this article.

The spreadsheet is available for download as a stand-alone .xlsm file. Many cells in the spreadsheet are protected, hidden, and/or validated to maintain the integrity of the spreadsheet. In addition, the VBA project environment is also password protected, as are each of the worksheet tabs. However, you may still use the worksheets interactively, by entering data into the blue cells and using the macro buttons.

To download the .xlsm file, go to the following page on TraderEdge.net: https://traderedge.net/oshrm-spreadsheets/ and follow the download instructions.

You may need the *case-specific password* to *download* the Excel file. If required, the password to *download* the Excel file is: OSHRM3321

Once downloaded, you will also need the *case-specific password* to *open* the Excel file. The password required to *open* the Excel file is: OSHRM987

If the Trader Edge website is not accessible, please send an email *with an explanation of the specific error* received to (BJohnson@TraderEdge.Net). *Include your copy of the electronic receipt* for the purchase of this book and I will send you a copy of the .xlsm file as an email attachment.

Given the complexity of the spreadsheets and macros, it is possible that a few coding or formula errors survived the debugging process. If so, it is likely that these will be discovered after publication. Please send me an email with a detailed description of any coding or formula errors that meet *both of the following criteria*:

1. IS reproducible in the *latest version of Microsoft Excel*.

2. IS NOT a function of a specific set of user data or input values.

As explained earlier, the Terms tab includes a partial disclaimer and a link to the full terms and conditions on the TraderEdge.Net site that govern the use of the spreadsheet. The user must read and agree to all of the terms and conditions before using the workbook. The workbook will not function unless the terms and conditions have been explicitly accepted.

Until those terms are explicitly accepted, many spreadsheet cells will appear to contain errors: "#VALUE!" These are not spreadsheet errors. The macros and spreadsheet calculations will not function correctly until the terms have been explicitly accepted. The "#VALUE!" messages can also occur when first opening the spreadsheet. If these "#VALUE!" messages ever occur (for any reason), accept the terms on the Terms tab *and then enter a new (different) value in one or more of the blue user input cells to force all of the "#VALUE!" cells to recalculate.* If these steps do not resolve the problem, the error is probably data-specific.

I do not offer user spreadsheet support or investment advice. However, if I can replicate and correct a structural (non-data-specific) OSHRM spreadsheet error, I will upload a corrected copy of the spreadsheet to the Trader Edge download page and I will update the file origination date on the same page. Please check the download page periodically for the latest versions of the spreadsheets.

I hope you enjoy these tools and find them useful in your option trading and research.

Printed in Great Britain
by Amazon

22864342R00076